Comics Writing
Communicating
with Comic Books

Steven Philip Jones

Foreword by
Dan Jurgens

CALIBER COMICS   **Detroit**

To Christopher Jones
Great Talent
Better Friend

writing n. 1. the act of a person who writes 5. a book, poem, article, or other literary work 6. the profession or occupation of a writer 7. the art, style, etc. of literary composition

- Webster's New World Dictionary

For information address:

CALIBER ENTERTAINMENT
  www.calibercomics.info

Printed in the United States of America

By Steven Philip Jones

Comic Books & Graphic Novels

Alien Nation: A Breed Apart	‖ Mighty 1
August	Nightlinger
Carmilla	The People That Time Forgot
Curious Cases of Sherlock Holmes	Re-Animator
Dracula	Scales of the Dragon: "Vanguard"
Dracula: The Lady in the Tomb	Seduction: "Second Stringer"
Dracula: The Suicide Club	Street Heroes 2005
H. P. Lovecraft in Color	* Talismen: Calling the King
Halloween Horror: "Kin"	† Tatters
Invaders from Mars	Wolverstone & Davis: Street Heroes
Invaders from Mars II	Worlds of H.P. Lovecraft, Vol. 1&2

Novels & Novellas

Bushwhackers
‡ Henrietta Hex: Shadows from the Past
King of Harlem
Re-Animator: Tales of Herbert West
* The Sceptre: The Frigid Castle
* Talismen: The Knightmare Knife
* Talismen: The Boy in the Well
§ Teenage Mutants: White Knights & Raiders
Wizard Academies: The House with the Witch's Hat

Non-fiction

The Clive Cussler Adventures: A Critical Review
Comics Writing: Communicating with Comic Books

Radio Drama

Sherlock Holmes: Adventure of the Petty Curses
Sherlock Holmes: A Case of Unfinished Business

* with Barb Jacobs
† with Aldin Baroza
‡ with Shannon Denton
§ with Christopher Jones
‖ created by David D. Arnold
editor

CONTENTS

ACKNOWLEDGEMENTS

It's been a long ride. I'll do my best not to leave anyone out. If I do, sincerest apologies.

Thanks to…

…the friends who shared my dream: Dave Arnold, S. Clarke Hawbaker, Barb Jacobs, Christopher Jones, Mike Matthews, John Olson, Bill Rosell, Mark Stegbauer, and Dennis Stick.

…the kindred met along my journey: Aldin Baroza, Octavio Carillo, Sergio Carillo, Sandy Carruthers, Rob Davis, Phil Hester, Dan Jurgens, Ande Parks, John Ross, and Robert Schneiders.

…the folks who gave me a chance: Ed Gorman, Dave Olbrich, Tom Mason, and Gary Reed.

…the creators who kindled my love: John Byrne, Chris Claremont, Stephen Englehart, Steve Gerber, Archie Goodwin, Mike Grell, Marshall Rogers, Walt Simonson, and Al Williamson.

…the grandmasters who blazed my trail: Steve Ditko, Will Eisner, Bill Finger, Bob Kane, Gil Kane, Jack Kirby, Thomas Nast, Stan Lee, and Charles Schultz.

…the scholars who carried the torch for me: Will Eisner (again), Randall P. Harrison, R.C. Harvey, and Scott McCloud.

…the inspirations who show me how: Richard Bach, Ray Bradbury, Clive Cussler, Brian Daley, Sir Arthur Conan Doyle, Alain-Fournier, Dashiell Hammett, Robert A. Heinlein, Stephen King, H. P. Lovecraft, Edgar Allan Poe, Rafael Sabatini , Carl Sagan, and Bram Stoker.

…the teachers who taught me how: Jay Holstein and J. Kenneth Kuntz.

…the family I love more than anything: Katie and Lisa.

No one does it alone. I couldn't have done it without you.

FOREWORD

We all know people who love comics. They'll speak with great passion about their favorite books and characters and, sometimes, with even greater passion about the books they dislike.

There are also those whose passion is rooted in analyzing and breaking down what they've read, because it allows them to understand the story in greater detail and precision. Those are the folks who key in on not just what the writer might have accomplished on the story's surface, but on a secondary level. They try to identify the writer's intent and progression, which is a whole other way of understanding comics.

One of those people is Steven Philip Jones.

When I first met Steven, longer ago than either of us would care to admit, his passion for comics was apparent. His affection for story deconstruction was even more obvious, as he was very clear and precise in speaking about what he liked and *why*.

It's because he took the time to do the hard work in coming to that understanding of the material.

Now, you have the chance to benefit from that hard work. Steven has done it for you, here, in crystal clear detail that will enhance your appreciation of the graphic storytelling medium that we all love so much.

Dan Jurgens
November, 2013

INTRODUCTION

Admit it. You really don't want to learn how to write comics. You want to know *what to do* so you can start writing comics *right now.*

Deny it if you want.

I know better.

Oh, yes, I know.

I found out the hard way many years ago, starting when I was asked to teach ninth-grade students about writing comic books at a young writer's conference.

Somewhere along the line I wrote a thirty-five page pamphlet called *The Comic Book Writer's Handbook* that the students could take home and refer to later, and after the conference I printed some extra copies to sell at comic book conventions. A couple of years later I was at the Kansas City Comic Show when a friend, comics artist Rob Davis (*Daughter of Dracula, Star Trek: Deep Space Nine*), asked if he could read my pamphlet. I was happy to give Rob one because he is that rarest combination of talents: a good creator and a good teacher. Rob can look at an artist's portfolio and in clear and simple terms explain what is good in the portfolio, what needs work, and what the artist can do to strengthen any weaknesses. Rob is so good at this that I have seen more popular artists sitting near him at conventions strain their ears to pick up tips. So you can bet I was excited to hear what Rob had to say about *The Comic Book Writer's Handbook.*

And Rob's opinion was, "It's okay. Pretty much just covers the basics, doesn't it?"

As usual Rob hit the nail on the head. I wrote my pamphlet for junior high school students wanting to learn about writing comic books, so I should have been gratified by Rob's evaluation, but I was disappointed. For some reason I had been hoping Rob would say, "Gee, Steve, this is one of the most perceptive analysis of comic book communication I have ever read."

Yeah.

Right.

In thirty-five pages no less.

Go figure.

Nevertheless I was disappointed and I inadvertently carried that disappointment over to a new adult education class I was teaching called *Introduction to Comic Book Writing.* Instead of teaching my first class what to do when it came to writing comic books I tried to teach them the in-depth information that would impress a professional like Rob Davis.

That was one boneheaded move.

Sixteen students signed up for that first eight-week *Introduction to Comic Book Writing* class, and by the final week four students or 25% of the total had dropped out.

Way to go, Steve.

I don't want to make that mistake with this book, so let me tell you up front that **my goal with *Comics Writing* is to get you up to speed on the basics of writing comics so you can start writing them as quickly as possible. Nothing more, but nothing less.** And by "basics" I mean the nuts and bolts of comics and writing along with one or two little tricks of the trade.

Now let me turn the tables for a moment and warn you about a mistake you might be making with this book.

Is reading *Comics Writing* going to turn you into a comic book writer?

No.

All this book can do is tell you what to do. If you want to become a comics writer then you are going to have to take the information and suggestions presented here and try them.

And try them.

And try them again.

You know what I am talking about. Practice!

Of course no one can make you practice, but there is no getting around the fact that practice is still the only way to get to Carnegie Hall.

That said, becoming a comics writer takes more than trying and trying and trying. You can practice writing for years and never improve unless you have something to say and an unstoppable desire to try to say it. And please don't confuse "having something to say" with writing *Moby Dick.* I'm not talking about anything so ambitious or complicated. Most comics readers want entertainment, not insights into **LIFE'S BIG QUESTIONS,** so successful writers write about things that delight or deject or outrage them. Successful writers have fun when they write, even when they write about distasteful or tragic things. They have fun because they write with zest and gusto, and their stories transmit that fun to their readers.

I write comics stories because 1) I love to write and 2) I love comics, not because I hope to make millions of dollars. Rich comics writers are as rare as hen's teeth. And I don't write comics stories to become the center of attention at comic book conventions. I like my privacy just fine, thank you. Don't get me wrong, fortune and fame may be respectable goals, but there are easier ways to reach them then being a writer, especially a comics writer. Ernest Hemingway (*The Old Man and the Sea*, *For Whom the Bell Tolls*) was one of the most influential and successful authors of the 20th Century, but when he delivered his acceptance speech for the Noble Prize for Literature in 1954 he

How long has it been since you wrote a story where your real love or your real hatred somehow got onto the paper? When was the last time you dared release a cherished prejudice so it slammed the page like a lightning bolt? What are the best things and worst things in your life, and when are you going to get around to whispering or shouting them?
- Ray Bradbury

made a point of stressing that writing is difficult and lonely. So before reading any further, ask yourself, "Do I want to write? Or do I want to have written?" There is a very serious difference.

Oh, one more thing. Even if you master the craft of comics writing there is no guarantee that you will earn a living doing it.

Sorry.

You are going to have to take your chances like the rest of us.

Now if all this hasn't blunted your enthusiasm to learn the craft of comics writing, and if you are willing to risk the time and effort to learn comics writing if only someone would tell you how to get started, then congratulations! You have come to the right place because that is what I intend to do.

And the best time for us to get started is right now.

PART ONE: COMICS

1) COMICS

A comics writer does two things.

1) Entertains readers by creating stories.

2) Communicates his stories so that collaborators can translate them into comics.

There you go. What could be simpler?

Before we proceed, though, let me ask a question.

What is "comics"?

Now you might be thinking, "Puh-leaze, fool! Comics are things like comic books, graphic novels, newspaper comic strips, webcomics, and digital comics! Everybody knows that!"

That comes close to hitting the bull's-eye, but close only counts in dancing and collateral damage. Frank Miller, the creator of *Dark Knight Returns* and *Sin City*, puts steel on target when he states, "Comics is, foremost, a form of communication."

Comics is a **medium**, a unique form of communication.

Comics is **narrative art** that uses words and pictures to communicate.

And comics is a member of the **cartoon family tree** with its own communication code called the grammar of comics that cartoon communication expert Randall P. Harrison says writers and artists use "to create a make-believe world, to create figures, to give them depth, to give them action, thought, and language."

Comics as a Medium

A medium conveys information, rather it is news or ideas, in a method unlike any other medium. Comics is often compared to film because both are verbal-visual media that use words and pictures to convey information, but this is a flawed comparison. Film is an audio-visual medium that uses sound and moving images to communicate, whereas comics has no soundtrack or moving images but uses static words and images. While comics is a verbal-visual medium like film, it would be more accurate to compare comics to literary media like books, newspapers, and magazines.

Comics as Narrative Art

Narrative art is one of mankind's oldest forms of communication. According to Harrison, "Cartoons, and even strip-like stories, can be found in Roman sculpture, on Greek vases, on early Japanese scrolls, and in the famous Bayeux tapestry." The Pyramid of Khufu is the oldest of Egypt's trademark pyramids, finished in 2530 B.C., but one of the earliest examples of narrative art is almost two hundred years older than that. The Standard of Ur is an ancient box with shell-inlaid figures and images on its outside depicting a Sumerian military action and subsequent victory. According to the popular textbook *Gardner's Art Through the Ages* these "figures are carefully arranged in superimposed strips, each strikingly suggestive of a film or 'comic strip'; doubtless, the purpose is the same—to achieve a continuous narrative effect." Ancient people had discovered that they could record historical events in greater detail by combining words with images into narrative art than with art or writing alone.

Comics as Cartoon

The word **cartoon** is over five hundred years old. It comes from the French and Italian words for "card" and "paper." Until 1455 the word "cartoon" was used to describe a preliminary sketch for a painting or sculpture, but after the invention of movable type made printing presses all the rage in Western European "cartoon" was used to describe any sketch that could be mass-produced.

These early cartoons were very simple to make reproducing them on printing presses easier. They were also very simplistic in nature, but today any drawing is considered to be a cartoon regardless of its complexity so long as it encapsulates a complete thought. In plain English, this means that any illustration can be called a cartoon.

Two Definitions for Comics

Which brings us back to my question, "What is comics?"

Believe it or not there is no single agreed-upon definition for comics, despite the best efforts of two of the most knowledgeable comics communicators of the last century to create one.

During the Seventies comics grandmaster Will Eisner (*The Spirit, A Contract With God*) coined the term "sequential art" to describe the medium. Sequential art is piquant and to the point but fails to describe the comics medium to anyone who has never seen anything like a comic book or a comic strip. For this reason Scott McCloud expanded the term sequential art into a proper dictionary-style definition for his milestone text on comics communication, *Understanding Comics* (1993). What he came up with was:

> Juxtaposed pictorial and other images in deliberate sequence intended to convey information and/or produce an aesthetic response in the reviewer.

Intimidating, isn't it? I know it scares the heck out of me.

My problem with McCloud's definition, besides inducing brain cramps, is that it fails to mention words as an element of comics, even though comics is narrative art and a verbal-visual medium.

My Definition of Comics (Sort Of)

For this book I have attempted to cobble a more precise description of the comics medium than what Eisner or McCloud created. The components come from one of the first critical examinations of the medium, Coulton Waugh's *The Cartoon* (1947). Waugh argued that all comics had to include three criteria: 1) A narrative told through a sequence of pictures, 2) a continuing cast of characters, and 3) the inclusion of dialogue or text within the cartoon. Technically a continuing cast of characters is in no way necessary to communicate anything in any medium, so I have taken the liberty of scrapping this criterion and connecting the remaining criteria to assemble the following:

> *COMICS*: A narrative told through a sequence of pictures with the inclusion of dialogue or text within the cartoon.

There is your answer, Charlie Brown. That is what comics is all about.

2) BREAKING DOWN THE CODE

Okay, what do you need to know about the comics medium to write comics? In *The Cartoon: Communication to the Quick* (1981) Harrison lists five types of cartoons:

- **The cartoon illustration**
- **The single-panel cartoon**
- **The narrative art cartoon**
- **The animated cartoon**
- **The cartoon product**

These types represent the five branches of the cartoon family tree.

A **cartoon illustration** is any drawing that illustrates text that is surrounding it. These days cartoon illustrations can be found in many instruction manuals, technical books, and young adult adventure and humor novels.

The **single-panel cartoon** is a drawing that is combined with words. So long as these words operate as part of the cartoon they can appear anywhere near or in the drawing. Examples of single-panel cartoons include *The Far Side* and *Dennis the Menace*. The **narrative art cartoon** (which includes the comics medium) is a sequence of drawings that incorporate words within the artwork. These words typically appear in speech balloons and caption boxes.

An **animated cartoon** incorporates a soundtrack to communicate words, sound effects, and music. Unlike the cartoon illustration, single-panel cartoon, or narrative art cartoon the drawings in the animated cartoon appear to move.

The fifth cartoon type, the **cartoon product,** is an umbrella term that refers to different ways comics are licensed and marketed, from *Peanuts* figurines to *Mallard Fillmore* notepads to *Heavenly Nostrils* tees to *Pearls Before Swine* calendars to Opus the Penguin stuffed animals to … well, I think you get the idea.

Three Things All Cartoon Types Have in Common

The three ingredients these five cartoon types share in common are content, complexity, and code.

Content is what a cartoon is about. The content of the newspaper strip *Garfield* is about the misadventures of a lasagna-loving fat cat who rarely thinks of anyone except himself, while the content of the Pixar animated film *The Incredibles* (2004) is about a family of superheroes searching for a purpose and a place in a world that has become unsure if superheroes can be trusted.

Complexity refers to how simple or complex a cartoon is when compared to other cartoons. For example, the complexity of the message, the design, even the production of a newspaper strip such as *Garfield* is far less then an animated cartoon such as *The Incredibles*.

Code is the most important communication tool employed by any cartoon. In communication *a code is used to transform information from one form into another form*, such as speech into writing or vice versa. As Harrison puts it, the cartoon code transforms "ideas and perceptions into pictorial and verbal symbols." Another name for the cartoon code is the **grammar of comics**.

If just the thought of grammar has a narcoleptic effect on you, try to stay awake as I ask you to remember two important things.

First, grammar is a system of rules for the use of language.

Second, grammar is the method used to structure the **elements** of a code.

If you are still awake, let us look at the English language for a moment. Words are the elements that are structured into the sentences we use to communicate. Nouns, pronouns, case, verbs, adjectives, adverbs, prepositions, and conjunctions are the grammatical terms boring English teachers use to explain the function and relationship of the words in a sentence, while subject and predicate, phrases, and clauses are the grammatical terms they use to identify and explain the parts of a sentence.

Cartoon communication is its own language with its own code and its own elements, and the grammar of comics is nothing more than the arrangement of those elements in sequence.

The Four Basic Graphic Elements of Comics

A comics writer is a cartoon communicator, a person who knows how to communicate using the grammar of comics. As British comics editor and writer Alan McKenzie (*Doctors Who, The Boxer*) puts it, "It is the writer's and artist's job to supply the reader with a stream of panels which show selected highlights from the action of a story." This process of selecting highlights is called narrative breakdown and it is one of the four basic graphic elements of the cartoon code along with layout, composition, and style.

Narrative breakdown is the process of taking a story (the narrative) and breaking it down into a series of panels.

Composition refers to the size and shape of a panel as well as what appears inside the panel. A panel can be as large or as small on a page as your need and you can show anything inside a panel that an artist can draw.

Layout is the arrangement of panels on a page. You can arrange panels any way you want on a page, but a good layout is easy for the reader to understand. In the United States and other Western countries, panels proceed in a left to right progression from the top of a page to the bottom in a series of **rows** or **tiers**.

As for **style**, it is the way an artist's work looks or the sound a writer's words make on paper.

The four basic graphic elements at work on Page 1 of *Little Dragon: Chapter One*.

"You Are About to Enter A Dimension of Time and Space"

Two key ingredients are required if you are going to make narrative breakdown, composition, layout, and style work, and they are **Time** and **Space**.

All stories are a sequence of incidents in time. A story begins at a specific point in time and ends at another specific point in time, and the events that take place between those points make up your story. Time in turn sets up **viewpoint**, which *locates*, *focuses*, *limits*, and *defines* the space of a story. If there is no viewpoint the reader will feel as lost as a prisoner in an isolation cell who has no notion of night and day. The reader must know when and where a story takes place as well as when the incidents in a story occur in relation to one another. One of the easiest ways to establish and maintain viewpoint is through a **viewpoint character** that witnesses the events of the story. A viewpoint character serves as the reader's eyes, ears, nose, mouth, and hands, much like a camera does in a movie. Viewpoint characters can be a main character or one of your minor characters. It does not matter. The only qualification a viewpoint character has to have is that he sees all the action in a story for the reader.

With that in mind, narrative breakdown creates a sense of time in a comics story. Again, a story is a sequence of incidents in time, and since narrative breakdown breaks a story down into a sequence of panels those panels act as indicators (events) that time is being divided at a pace that the reader may not perceive but will definitely appreciate.

Layout varies the placement, size, and shape of panels on a page, all of which enhances the story by manipulating time and space. For example a series of narrow panels running together in a row can suggest a rapid passage of time, while long vertical panels can suggest a slower passage of time.

Composition likewise takes advantage of variety to enhance drama, only in this case we are talking about variety in a panel's visual elements such as distance and camera angles. "The idea," writes McKenzie, "is to get variety into the way which you present the sequence." McKenzie adds that variety also prevents uncomfortable eyestrain for the reader, "So it is best to make sure that you do not create a sequence that is all close-ups or all long shots."

The female protagonist Taym is the viewpoint character in Pages 2 & 4 from *Little Dragon: Chapter Two*. Her memories guide the reader through Time and Space, beginning with some unexplained important event in the past on her homeworld and then through her formal education and martial training.

To get a better idea of what McKenzie means let us look at a page from the webcomic *Talismen: Return of the Exile*. This page shows a U.S. Marine, Lance Corporal Ollie Steele, who finds himself inexplicably transported away from terrorist captors to the sanctuary of a dreamland where he meets an elflike warrior girl named Astrina. Barb Jacobs not only drew this page but also plotted it and created the narrative breakdown, and she does an excellent job of employing variety in her layout and composition.

Panel 1 is a close-up of Ollie and Astrina (CU 2-shot) with the camera's perspective focused upon Ollie. Since this is the first time Ollie's face appears it is important that the reader gets a good look at him as Ollie tries to grasp his sudden change of scenery.

Panel 2 is seen from Astrina's point-of-view (POV) as she cuts Ollie's bonds, visually accentuating his release even as Astrina's dialogue keeps pushing the story forward.

Panels 3 and 4 are both full shots (FS) that feature a lot of dialogue, but there is also variety thanks to the changes in the camera angle in Panel 3 to Panel 4. The camera also pans in closer in Panel 4 as the reader learns more about what is happening.

The page ends in Panel 5 with a CU from Ollie's POV. This camera angle puts the reader in Ollie's shoes, so to speak, as Astrina conveys what sounds like impossible information.

How a writer or an artist manipulates Time and Space using narrative breakdown, layout, and composition is a part of that creator's individual style.

Style is the sum total of a person's efforts to communicate and for my money one of the best explanations for this process is this one by Nelson Glenn McCrea, a professor of Latin Language and Literature at Columbia University:

> The object of language is to convey thought and feeling from one mind to another without loss of moving power. Style as it seems to me, is that form into which one may cast his conception with reasonable confidence that because of this form his conception will be able to operate without friction; i.e., without loss of power. If in mechanics force be applied in an improper way, either the work will not be done at all, or, if done, will be accomplished only with great waste of energy. If style is adequate, the idea will have free play, and will gain power to move.

Nine Unique Elements to Cartoon Communication

Along with the four basic elements of the grammar of comics, there are nine other elements unique to cartoon communication that are necessary for comics writing:

- format
- panels (a.k.a frame)
- panel borders
- closure
- artwork
- word balloons (a.k.a. speech balloons and thought balloons)
- caption boxes
- sound effects
- symbolia

Formats are the different types of comics. Comic books, comic strips, graphic novels, webcomics, and digital comics are all different comics formats.

A **panel** or **frame** shows one of the story's selected highlights. Most comic book panels are rectangular, but a panel can be drawn in any shape so long as the reader can understand what is happening inside the panel and follow the story.

Most panels are delineated by **panel borders** that can be drawn in different ways to communicate storytelling information. For example panels with wavy borders will have a dreamy or hallucinogenic sensation while hectic zigzagging borders give a panel a sense of dire urgency.

McCloud calls **closure** "the heart of comics" and McKenzie explains why closure is so important:

> [Comics] tell a story and thus they have to depict the passage
> of time ... Between frames, the creators and the readers
> 'agree' that an amount of time, of some particular duration,
> has passed as the strip is read from left to right (and down
> the page, if necessary).

To this McCloud adds that, "Critics tend to see only what's in the panels—not what's between them. And what's between them is the *only* element of comics that is not duplicated in any other medium." Closure is the element that makes comics unique. McCloud continues, "Comic panels fracture both time and space, offering a jagged, staccato rhythm of unconnected moments. But closure allows us to connect these moments and mentally construct a continuous, unified reality."

Artwork refers to the images that appear inside a panel. This may sound like another term for composition, but when it comes to cartoon communication it is the element of "artwork" that gives the artist direct contact with the reader, the same way **word balloons** and **caption boxes** give the writer direct contact to the reader. Artists communicate to the reader by the way they draw (visually execute) a scene, while writers communicate necessary story information not conveyed by the artwork (such as what characters say, think, or feel) to the reader. These tasks sound like two separate operations, but they must function together for the verbal-visual medium of comics to be successful.

Sound effects represent important noises that the cartoon communicator wants the reader to be aware of during a story, such as the eerie *creeeeaaak* of a door in the deserted attic of a spooky house or the metallic *tippa-tippa-tippa* of a tap-dancer's shoes cascading across a stage. Sound effects are most often used to move the story along or establish a mood. Most artists leave the job of drawing sound effects in a panel to the letterer, but there are design-minded artists like Eisner, Walt Simonson, Howard Chaykin, Marshall Rogers, Dan Jurgens, and Christopher Jones who integrate sound effects into their compositions, actually making the sound effect a part of the scenery and in essence a part of the story.

Symbolia is a pseudo-academic term coined by comic strip artist Mort Walker (*Beetle Bailey, Hi & Lois*) to refer to the unique icons cartoonists have invented to communicate non-verbal actions and sensations. Walker defines a few of these symbolia in his book *Lexicon of Comicana* (1980) including *waftarom* (wavy lines to show the aroma of cooking food), *dites* (diagonally straight lines to indicate a mirror or window pane), *hites* (horizontal lines used to produce the illusion of speed), *agitrons* (lines emanating from a character's head to indicate surprise), and *plewds* (drops of sweat flying off a person's head to indicate a variety of different emotions).

And there you go. The grammar of comics.

Now the time has come to take these elements out of their boxes and put them to work to see what they can do.

ART NOTES
Page 14: Nightlinger sketch by Christopher Jones © 2014
Pages 16-17: *Little Dragon #1*, art & letters by Rob Davis © 1996
Page 18: *Talismen: Return of the Exile* by Barb Jacobs © 2005

3) A CARTOON CODE AUTOPSY

To see the grammar of comics in action, let us perform a cartoon code autopsy. Call me mad, but I think it just might help.

On pages 23-26 you will find Pages 1-4 from *Nightlinger #1*. For those unfamiliar with *Nightlinger* the titular character Feril Nightlinger is a classic pulp-style mystery man. The world's foremost illusionist and escape artist, Nightlinger is also a modern-day knight errant who, with the aid of his beautiful, athletic, and quick-witted assistant Michael "Mike" Segretto, helps people plagued by problems that more often than not are supernatural in nature.

Narrative Breakdown

The narrative takes place in and under a rural New England cemetery during the dead of night. Mike Segretto is hiding in a conifer, watching someone (Nightlinger) exhume a grave. One moment the digger is standing in the grave. The next, he vanishes. Segretto investigates and discovers the grave's coffin has a hole where its bottom should be. She jumps through the hole and finds a tunnel beneath the grave. Segretto follows the sounds of gunfire out of the tunnel into the cyclopean ruins of a subterranean city filled with unearthly eikons and non-Euclidean structures.

These four pages are divided into nineteen panels.

There is one panel on Page 1, seven panels on Page 2, eight panels on Page 3, and three panels on Page 4.

Page 1 introduces the story with a large single panel called a **splash page**. The first page of any comic book must engage or hook someone into wanting to read more, like the opening sentence of a novel or a short story, and for this reason kicking off a story with a splash page was once routine in comic books because very few things shout *Readmereadmereadme!* like a big flashy picture.

Page 2 focuses on Segretto spying on Nightlinger, beginning with an **establishing shot** of the graveyard in Panel 1. We get our first good look at Segretto in Panel 2. Panels 3-4 are both POV shots from Segretto's perspective. Panels 5-7 show Segretto moving from conifer to grave.

Page 3 focuses on Segretto's actions above and in the tunnel. Panels 1 and 3 concentrate on Segretto. They also buttress Panel 2 which shows the coffin. Segretto enters the tunnel in Panel 4, searches for Nightlinger in Panels 5-6, and hears the off-panel gunfire in Panel 7. In Panel 8 Segretto follows the sound towards a brilliant light.

Page 4 focuses on Segretto discovering the terrible ruins. Panels 1-2 are inserted near the top of Panel 3, a splash page, with Panel 1 showing Segretto reaching the end of the tunnel and Panel 2 concentrating on Segretto's wide eyes. Panel 3 is an imposing view of the cyclopean ruins.

Layout

A layout should never be a haphazard collection of panels on a page. The primary purpose of a layout is to guide the eye through a page from one panel to the next without confusing the reader. The layouts on Pages 1-4 are straightforward in their

Writer and artist Mike Grell does the splash page one better in his series The Warlord. *The narrative for the first page of each story is broken down into more than one panel. Page 1 quickly sets up the action, and then Pages 2-3 feature a panoramic single panel called a double-page spread. These double-page spreads are a signature of* The Warlord.

arrangements, but also sophisticated in that all nineteen panels are coordinated to perform as a four-page unit that present the prologue to *Nightlinger* #1.

The splash pages on Pages 1 and 4 function as bookends for Pages 2 and 3. These two middle pages are each divided into three rows or tiers, with the top tier establishing its page's setting, Page 2 in the graveyard and Page 3 under the graveyard.

The top tier of Page 2 consists of one wide panel and its bottom tier has three panels, while Page 3 flops this arrangement, with three panels in its top tier and a wide panel (that includes a circular **insert panel** on the left) in its bottom tier. Furthermore, the middle tier on Pages 2 and 3 both include the same unorthodox three-panel arrangement: one panel on the left with two smaller panels stacked on the right.

Composition

The composition on Page 1 showcases the *Nightlinger* series logo along with two vertical borders of intertwined snakes running across the top and sides of the single panel. Both the logo and the borders are rendered in a Celtic style that imbues the story with a mythical essence, while the Nightlinger character is introduced as a powerful but haunting spectral image glowering over "an aberrant megalithic structure brooding over its primordial secrets." Everything inside the panel is drawn in a representative art style *except* the scroll-shaped caption box in the upper right corner, which is drawn in an abstract medieval style. The caption box's anachronistic style, shape, unique lettering (typeset instead of handwritten), and location on the page suggest that this caption is a separate but exceptional piece of the story. Which it is, as we discover when we read its copy, a quote from H. P. Lovecraft's "The Thing on the Doorstep" borrowed to introduce the series' theme.

A transition technique similar to a motion picture cross-fade occurs on Pages 1-2. The full moon, in all its cliché spooky glory, is positioned in the upper left corner of both pages, but the moon is smaller and placed a bit higher on Page 2, demonstrating that location, time, or both have changed from Page 1. This transition technique works because the full moon is the first object we notice on Page 2. Since people in Western cultures read a page from left to right, we notice the full moon first on Page 2 because it is in the upper left corner of Panel 1. From there the eye moves across the page to the right, cuts back to the left and down, and then across the page right again in a zigzag track until it reaches the bottom.

The artist and letterer, Aldin Baroza, composed these panels to assist the eye along this zigzag path. In Panel 1 if you laid a ruler across Segretto's shoulder blades and down her left arm, you could draw a straight line—the same line the eye travels as it zags down the page—to Segretto's right arm and elbow in Panel 2. Next, because of the unusual vertical arrangement of Panels 3-4, Baroza is careful to steer the reader in the right direction by having Segretto scratch the bridge of her nose using her right index finger. (Is she just scratching or could she be sneaking a point towards Panel 3?) In Panel 3 the position of Nightlinger's body drags the eye down to Panel 4, where it can resume its natural zigzag track to Panel 5.

On Page 3 not only the composition but the layout calls attention to the suffocating subterranean confines in Panel 4. Segretto's surroundings force her to bend over while the panel is surrounded by the page's other panels, an enclosure that creates a sense of claustrophobia. The only "opening" appears to be on the left behind Segretto, but when Segretto turns around in Panel 5 to look in that direction she sees nothing but more tunnel, an observation that is repeated when she turns around again in Panel 6.

Page 4 is the antithesis of Page 3. Still subterranean, this page forsakes claustrophobia for agoraphobia. Segretto has escaped the dark and suffocating tunnel in Panel 1 only to find herself in the mammoth cavern and the bizarre cyclopean ruins in Panel 3.

Style

Style, you may remember, is the way an artist's work looks or the sound a writer's words make on paper, as well as the sum total of a person's efforts to communicate. Style should be distinctive. A style can be easily identifiable (e.g., painter Frank Frazetta, novelist Raymond Chandler), but any one style can be difficult to describe. It is a simple thing to watch the technique of a camera panning in on an open window in a film and comment, "That looks like a Hitchcock shot," but it is much harder to explain why such shots are evocative of Hitchcock's idiosyncratic style.

I may not be able to adequately describe my writing style or Baroza's art style in words, but I can tell you that the execution of each element we have examined in *Nightlinger* #1 so far is a part of the sum total that makes up mine and Baroza's styles. Other ingredients such as the words I compose for each character to speak or the way Baroza draws faces and anatomy also go into our styles. These ingredients also include my and Baroza's unique personalities, the individual strengths and weaknesses we each possess, and the fact that different writers and artists will want to emphasize different story highlights and storytelling elements in their work. All of this goes into creating style.

Unless a writer or artist is intentionally aping someone else's style, no two people draw or write exactly the same way. If another writer and artist, say someone like Frank Miller, had written and drawn these four pages he would not have used the same narrative breakdown, layout, and composition as Baroza and I. For example Miller draws faces and anatomy differently than Baroza, so Nightlinger and Segretto would not look the same. At the same time if Baroza had drawn one of Frank Miller's *Daredevil* stories it would look fundamentally different. (To see visual examples of how two different artists can handle the same script see Appendix.)

Time & Space

Besides being the key ingredients that make the four basic graphic elements of comics work, Time and Space are totally subjective in any comics story. Action in a story takes place at the same speed that a reader reads it, so (as McKenzie alludes to in the previous chapter) it is up to the creator(s) of a comics story to communicate how much time passes between each panel. Since Time and Space are subjective, however, they are as elastic in comics as they are relative in science ... or to put it more simply, Time and Space can be manipulated for storytelling effect. In fact few storytelling effects can be as simultaneously understated and powerful as messing with Time and Space.

In *Nightlinger* #1 Segretto finds herself engaged in an ancient hero motif known as the **descent into darkness**. To demonstrate what this is let us compare Segretto's descent with one experienced by a more famous heroine, Lewis Carroll's titular character from *Alice's Adventures in Wonderland*. In both of these stories a viewpoint character journeys from the land of reality into an incredible otherworld by *descending* into a *dark* underground where Time and Space become unpredictable.

In Carroll's novel, Alice pursues the White Rabbit down a rabbit hole before falling into a deep well where she seems to plummet for many hours. Alice falls asleep, dreams, and lands unharmed in a tunnel where she discovers a ten-inch door that opens out to a wondrous otherworld. Alice is too big to pass through the door, but finding a bottle with the label "Drink Me" she swallows its contents despite the realistic fear that the bottle could contain poison. Instead of dying she shrinks enough to enter Wonderland.

In *Nightlinger* #1, Segretto pursues her White Rabbit (i.e., Nightlinger) into the tunnel beneath the grave. Notice that in Page 2, Panel 1 there are several yards separating Segretto's conifer from the grave. In Panels 1-4 the uninterrupted tempo of Segretto's thought balloons—like the steady beat of a metronome—indicate that the action in the story is taking place at the same speed that we are reading the panels, but in Panels 5-7 Time and Space telescopes as Segretto's descent commences. We know this because Panels 5-7 form a **polyptych panel** that splits one large scene into three panels to show successive movements by the same character (Segretto) in different parts of this scene. Polyptych panels are commonly used to show a progression of human action within a common background or to isolate important scenes in a large panel. Here in Panels 5-7 the continuous treeline running along the background—coupled with the uninterrupted tempo of Segretto's thought balloons—indicate that unlike Panel 1 only a few feet now separate the conifer from the grave.

Panels & Closure

Panels and closure can also be used to manipulate Time and Space.

Remember how Alice and Segretto both experienced a change in Time as they began their descents into darkness? In Alice's case there was an expansion of Time (i.e., her impossibly long plummet), but for Segretto there was a telescoping of Time (i.e., the shrinking space between Segretto's tree and the grave from Panel 1 and Panels 5-7).

Both characters, though, experienced an increase in Space (i.e., they shrink) before leaving the darkness and entering their respective otherworlds. In Segretto's case on Page 3, Panel 4 she is forced to bend over at the waist when she first enters the tunnel under the grave, but in Panels 5-6 she can stand erect, and she continues to grow smaller in relation to her surroundings (Page 3, Panel 8 and Page 4, Panel 1) until she is dwarfed by the cyclopean ruins on Page 4, Panel 3.

Word Balloons & Caption Boxes

Words are as important as images in comics, and where word balloons and captions boxes are placed in a panel is vitally important. As Harrison explains, "The words reveal personality, and the proximity of word and figure, the simultaneous word and action, combine to give both immediacy and depth." The placement of word balloons and caption boxes can contribute or wreck layout and composition. For example notice that the caption box in Page 2, Panel 1 is placed so that it appears to flow away from the full moon like a cloud. This placement adds to Panel 1's eerie atmosphere even as it guides the eye rightward across the page.

Sound Effects & Symbolia

The only sound effects on these pages are the gunshots that appear in Page 3, Panel 7, but there are two examples of symbolia. The first is a pair of curved *hites* that indicate Segretto's leap out of the tree in Page 2, Panel 5. The second example is the *lightbeam* emanating from Segretto's flashlight on Page 2, Panel 7 and Page 3, Panels 5-6, and then from the ruins' cavern on Page 3, Panel 8 and Page 4, Panel 1. These lightbeams also serve a subliminal secondary purpose. Starting in Page 3, Panel 2 Segretto's flashlight corresponds with Segretto's POV. Page 2, Panel 7 and Page 3, Panels 1 & 3 establish this by showing Segretto shining her flashlight where she needs to see, while Page 3, Panel 2 is a true POV shot illuminated by the flashlight. Segretto's flashlight allows her to pierce the tunnel's darkness, which in turn allows Segretto to descend and search for figurative and literal illumination (i.e., knowledge). This descent into darkness/search for illumination subtext is accentuated by having Segretto appear in silhouette in every panel with a lightbeam.

All Done. Now That Wasn't So Bad, Was It?

There you have it. All the elements of the grammar of comics—the cartoon code that comic book creators use to communicate a story to the reader—in action.

Now the time has come to take a look at the collaborators a comics writer works with as well as a comics writer's most important tool when it comes to communicating a comics story to collaborators: the script.

ART NOTES
Page 22: *Nightlinger* #2, art & letters by Aldin Baroza, © 1993
Pages 23-26: *Nightlinger* #1, art & letters by Aldin Baroza, © 1993

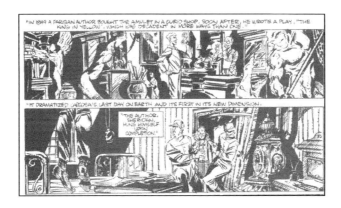

4) THE COLLABORATIVE PROCESS & THE SCRIPT

In novels, short stories, and other verbal literature a writer tells his story to the reader, but in verbal-visual media like comics the writer has to break his story down into some sort of script for his collaborators.

Comic book collaborators fall into four categories:

- sponsor
- writer
- artist
- editor

Comics is a mass medium and mass media are economic enterprises. Professional creators must be paid for their contributions to a comic book, editors require a regular paycheck to stay on the job, and print shop owners prefer to be paid in advance before rolling the presses on a hardcopy comic book. The responsibility for paying any bills falls to the **sponsor,** who takes a financial risk in hopes of receiving a profitable return on his investment. It is up to the **writer** to provide a story in the form of a script that is adapted into comics art by one or more artists. The duties of these **artists** are divided into the following roles:

Penciller: draws the story's images

Inker: goes over all pencils with black ink to accentuate depth and shadows during the printing process

Letterer: letters all dialogue, narration, and special effects as well as designs the story's title

Colorist: paints all the images with actual paint or computer software

The **editor** is the person responsible for a comics' production. It is the editor's job to get the writer and artist(s) to finish their work on schedule, to correct mistakes in a story's spelling, continuity, coloring, and pagination (order of pages), and for sending the finished story to the printer.

Each step of the collaborative process is vital to creating comics, but any endeavor that involves three, four, five, or more people is all but guaranteed to run into difficulties and confusion. So it is important that a writer does everything he can to make sure his collaborators can understand his contribution simply and quickly. This is why comics writers write their stories in the form of a script.

Three Different Script Styles to Chose From

In the movie business a script is called a *screenplay*. A television script is called a *teleplay*. Radio scripts are sometimes called *audio scripts*. In the theatre a script is called a *play*. Comics writers, perhaps a humbler breed than their counterparts in these other media, simply call the scripts they write a *script*.

There are as many different styles of comics scripts as there are comics writers. Over time the average comics writer will develop his own unique script style based upon his personality and work habits, but most comics scripts fall within the parameters of three basic formats: the plot-script, the full-script, and the Kurtzman-style script.

The **plot-script** is perhaps the most popular script format. Here the writer breaks down the story into individual pages but generally leaves layout and composition up to the artist. The writer is free to include narrative and dialogue, however most writers using a plot-script create copy for the captions and balloons after the story is drawn.

Writers who want to have more influence on how a story is drawn may prefer to use a **full-script** (my personal favorite). Here the writer breaks down the story page by page, panel by panel, describing the composition inside each panel and including all narrative and dialogue.

For writers wanting to maintain the most influence on how a story is drawn nothing beats a **Kurtzman-style script**. With this script, named after Harvey Kurtzman, editor of the classic EC Comics line of war titles like *Two-Fisted Tales*, the writer sketches the layout and composition of each page in "roughs" or "thumbnail sketches" (i.e., stick figure drawings). Captions and balloons can also be included if you want with narrative and dialogue written inside them. The artist then draws out the writer's roughs full-size. Not many writers use the Kurtzman-style script and most that do, like Frank Miller, Phil Hester (*Green Arrow*, *The Wretch*), and Archie Goodwin (*Manhunter*, *Star Wars*) are typically also artists, but non-artist writers like Mike Baron (*Nexus*, *The Badger*) have used this style with good results.

Which script format is best for you? That depends. Since the primary function of a script is to communicate your story, whichever format performs this function best for you and your collaborators is the one you should choose.

Example 1: The Plot-Script

In a plot-script the writer breaks the story down into individual pages and then describes what happens on each page. Below is a plot-script for Page One of *Mighty 1* #1:

PAGE ONE: The city of Manhattan as seen from New York harbor on a dazzling mid-July morning. The familiar skyline spans the horizon in BACKGROUND as boats and ferries of various sizes and styles travel in and out of the harbor.

A Liberty Island ferry is chugging through the harbor as water on one side of the ferry churns and bucks with waves.

In the largest panel on page FAFNIR, a colossal batrachian-humanoid monster (e.g., Godzilla, Cthulhu, or an Empire-State-Building-sized Creature From the Black Lagoon) erupts from the water. FAFNIR towers over the ferry, the Statue of Liberty appearing in BG to provide a scale of reference.

Example 2: The Full-Script

In a full-script the writer breaks the story into individual pages and then breaks each page into individual panels, describing each panel's composition and including any dialogue and narration. Below is a full-script for Page One of *Mighty* #1:

PAGE ONE:

Panel 1: EXT. DAY
PAGE-WIDE, THIN PANEL: ESTABLISHING SHOT of Manhattan as seen from New York harbor on a dazzling mid-July morning. The familiar skyline spans the horizon in BACKGROUND as boats and ferries of various sizes and styles travel in and out of the harbor.

CAP:
A warm and sunny summer morning
in the Gotham of Manhattan.

#2:
The start of another bustling work day.

Panel 2: FULL-SHOT
of a Liberty Island ferry as it chugs across the water of the harbor. On one side of the ferry the water is churning and starting to buck with waves. Passengers flock to this side of the ferry to gawk at what is happening and point down at the turbulence.

CAP:
Everything is as normal as can be.

#2:
Or—is it?

Panel 3: LONG-SHOT
LARGEST PANEL ON PAGE: FAFNIR, a colossal batrachian-humanoid monster (e.g., Godzilla, Cthulhu, or an Empire-State-Building-sized Creature From the Black Lagoon) erupts from the water. FAFNIR towers over the little ferry, the Statue of Liberty appearing in BG to provide a scale of reference.

Title: [MIGHTY 1 logo] in FREE PUBLICITY
Credits:

Example 3: The Kurtzman-Style Script

In a Kurtzman-style script a writer sketches each page of the story. The objective is to *show* an artist each page's layout and every panel's composition. The placement of balloons and captions can also be shown and the writer can jot the dialogue and narrative inside these placements or include them on a separate piece of paper. Below is a sample Kurtzman-style script sans balloons and captions for Page One of *Mighty* #1.

You may have noticed that my full-script incorporates a couple of screenplay terms like "establishing shot" and "full-shot." Comics is a literary medium, but many screenplay terms adapt well enough for use in comics scripts that it has become common practice for comics writers to borrow them when appropriate. (For more terms commonly used by comics writers in their scripts see Glossary.) Comics writer and artist Mary Wllshire (*Power Girl, Red Sonja*) explains that comics writers and artists will "speak often in camera terms, or movie terms … We use these camera terms, because really what [comics creators are] talking about a lot is cinematography. You're choosing the pictures that you want to use to tell the story best, which is what a cinematographer does." Even so it is important to remember that comics and movies are different media, a fact comics artist and comic book communication scholar R.C. Harvey stresses when he says that "however much these two media share, they are different in their essentials...[F]ilm is audio-visual while comics is purely visual; in comics, the eye takes in both word and picture."

Choosing the Format That's Best for You

The plot-script.
The full-script.
The Kurtzman-style script.
Which format is best for a beginning comics writer?

I would recommend the plot-script because it forces a writer to concentrate on breaking down a plot (a story element we will discuss in Chapter 9) and leaves layout and composition to the artist. Remember to keep your plot-script brief as lengthy plot-scripts can often be laborious and unnecessarily complicated for your collaborators. Simple and direct plot-scripts make it as easy as is possible for collaborators to understand what you are looking for in your story.

A full-script is better for a writer who is experienced enough and desires to take more control over how his story will be drawn. The basic format for a full-script makes it easy for an artist to work with while permitting a writer to concisely comment about action, atmosphere, dialogue, even a page's layout.

I would not recommend using a Kurtzman-style script until you feel confident with cartoon communication, but when you do feel ready it provides a benefit neither plot-scripts or full-scripts can offer. Communication science teaches that the best definition of any object is the *object itself*, while the second best definition is a *picture* of the object, and the third best is a verbal or written *description*. Plot-scripts and full-scripts are written *descriptions*, but a Kurtzman-style script is a *picture* of your story and how you would like to see it drawn. In other words a Kurtzman-style script is as close as you can get to drawing your story yourself without being the artist. The good news is that you do not have to be an artist to use a Kurtzman-style script. If you can draw boxes (for panels and captions), circles (for balloons), and stick figures (for stick figures) you are good to go.[1]

All recommendations aside, the best script format will always be the one that is most advantageous for you, your collaborators, and your team's schedule. No matter which format you decide to use, the primary function of a script remains the same: to communicate your story to your collaborators. A comics script tells a story but not in an entertaining way like a novel or a short story. It is a set of directions and suggestions for your collaborators to follow while they transform your story into comics artwork.

Whichever script format you use, you must describe your story so that everything is clear to your collaborator. Do not waste time fretting about whether your descriptions are deathless prose. What you must be concerned about is *clarity*. This cannot be overstressed. In the words of Jean Henri Fabre: "Clarity is the supreme politeness of him who wields the pen." Strive to make everything in your script easily understandable. When you have something to tell your artist, say it. Do not beat around the bush. And here is a good piece of practical advice that serves me well. Always let your collaborators know that they can contact you if they have any questions about anything in your script. Like writer-artist Mike Grell (*The Warlord, Jon Sable Freelance*) says, "Communication is the real key to working together. You're putting out a comic book and you're working together with a lot of people, and you have to talk, that's all there is to it."

The Collaborative Process (A Visual Review)

To take a closer look at what goes into creating a comic book story, let me walk you through the collaborative process for Page One of *Mighty 1 #1*. To do this we must first assume that the sponsor for *Mighty 1 #1* has agreed to pay to print this story in a hard copy comic book and that the script has received the green light from the editor.[2]

The editor is the first, last, and most overall involved person in the creative process of a comic book. An editor's main responsibility is to get a comic book ready for publication, and among his many tasks is deciding who will write and draw a comic book. The editor must have confidence not only in the talent and skill of a creator but in that creator's ability to complete an assignment on schedule. Comics is a mass medium and mass media have deadlines that must be met. It is also the editor's job to decide what idea will be accepted as a story for a comic book. Writers pitch story ideas to the editor, usually in the form of a short description called **springboards**.[3] An example of a springboard for *Mighty 1 #1* appears below:

> It is hardly news when a beautiful young 5'2" woman decides to tackle the fashion world. If she cold-cocks a fifty foot monster rampaging through New York City on national TV, that is news. Introducing Christina Puissant. But you can call her Mighty 1.

(For more examples of springboards see Chapter 13.)

After the script is written, the editor reads it to make sure that the plot makes sense, that the story flows well, that there are no holes in the logic or continuity, and that all dialogue and narration rings true. When the script receives final approval the editor sends it to the penciller, the artist who draws every page panel by panel.

When the pencils for the story are finished the penciller sends them to the editor, who checks them to make sure that characters have been accurately drawn, that the story has been translated correctly in the artwork, and that the

narrative breakdown not only makes sense but is easy for the reader to follow.

As soon as the pencils receive final approval they are sent to the inker, who may or may not be the same artist who pencils the story. Even with today's computer printing technology artwork that is inked prints much clearer and cleaner than pencil artwork, but inking is a tricky business because it cannot help but alter the original pencils.[4] The problem is that not every artist is as adept at inking as he is at penciling, and vice versa. Even if a

penciller is a good inker he may not be the best inker for his art. Another inker may be able to bring out desired qualities in the pencils that the original pencil artist cannot.

There is also the matter of time constraints. If a comic book is printed on a monthly schedule and if the penciller needs four weeks to pencil a story, then another four weeks to ink his pencils, an editor will have no choice but to limit that artist to the role of penciller.

In the halcyon days before computers engrained themselves into all facets

of our lives, it was common practice for pencil pages to be sent to the letterer before the inker. This is because all of the artwork for a page of a comic book story was drawn on the same sheet of Bristol board and it was more convenient for the letterer to pencil and ink all the word balloons, caption boxes, and sound effects over the pencil artwork (which could be removed by erasing) instead of inked artwork (which was permanent). With modern computer technology, however, it has become more expedient for the letterer to work over inked pages

that have been scanned into a computer. The inker can then email the finished lettered pages to the editor, who will proofread the pages against the original script. This was the case with *Mighty 1 #1*.

Not all comic book stories are colored. It is much cheaper to publish a comic book printed without colors, so most independent and small press comic books are black and white. When a book is colored, then the most common practice is to have the editor send scanned pages of the lettered artwork to a colorist or coloring team, who will color the artwork using a computer. Another option is to take the original artwork and transpose them into bluelines onto new art boards that are then sent to a painter who will color them using watercolors or oils.

Finally, the editor completes the collaborative process by taking the finished artwork and setting them into pagination along with any editorial pages, advertisements, and specialty pages before sanding this package and the comics' cover to the printer.

Time to Turn the Page

There is more to show you about the grammar of comics, the collaborative process, and scripts, but that can wait for now. The time has come to talk out about the single most important element of comics writing: the story.

ART NOTES
Page 32: *Nightlinger #2*, art & letters by Aldin Baroza © 1993
Pages 36 & 39: *Mighty 1 #1*, art by Christopher Jones © 1996

---

[1] Even though I do not use a Kurtzman-style script for my comics writing, I do sometimes include a sketch of a complex layout or a tricky panel composition with my plot-scripts and full-scripts. This is a trick of the trade that you may want to keep in mind while writing your scripts. Many of the artists I have worked with have told me they appreciate this extra effort.

[2] In the case of *Mighty 1* #1 the sponsor was Mighty 1's creator, David D. Arnold, who co-edited the story with John Olson. Olson also lettered the story.

[3] A springboard can be spoken or written, although it is more common to refer to a spoken springboard by its Hollywood term **elevator pitch**, so called because it can be presented in a very brief period of time, like during an elevator ride.

[4] When it comes to the importance of inking in comics communication, I agree with Professor James Kakalios. In his fascinating book *The Physics of Superheroes*, Professor Kakalios explains why he cites the writer and penciller but not the inker for the comic books he references in his book: "My omission of the inkers should not be construed as denigrating their contribution to the finished comic (I most certainly do not believe that such a job is equivalent to 'tracing'), but rather a reflection of the fact that the [penciller] along with the writer typically have the primary responsibility for the physics in a given comic book scene (p. xiv)."

PART 2: STORY

5) SOME PRELIMINARY STUFF

In a perfect world I would have started by discussing the subject of story instead of comics.

Why?

Because you have to know what a story is and how to write one before you can write a comics story.

So why didn't I do this?

I may not be the brightest crayon in the box, but eventually even I learn from my mistakes. When I taught my first adult education course on comic book writing I spent the entire first class covering the topic of story. This made perfect sense to me. Still does. It sounded perfectly boring to my students, though, all of whom thought they already knew everything there was about stories and just wanted to dive right into the subject of comics. If you read my introduction then you know how well things turned out with that first course. Since then whenever I teach comics writing I start by covering the subject of comics, just like I did in Chapters 1-4.

Well, bucko, this is chapter five and it's story time!

Time to Separate the Writers from the Posers

This is the moment when we separate the comics writers from the comics fan. From the person who sincerely yearns to learn how to write comics from the throng who just think writing comic book stories sounds cool and have no desire to work at the craft.

If you really want to be a writer—whether it is a comics writer or a novelist or a journalist or a copywriter—then all the elements of writing should be interesting to you. If you are serious about learning comics writing then learning the basics about writing a story should be interesting to you. If it is not then I suspect you will not be reading much more of this book.

If You're Going to Do It, Do It Right

"If there is one single thing wrong with comics today, it is the lack of good scripts." McKenzie wrote that statement in 1987 and it is as true today as it was then. Ditto McKenzie's assessment of why: "This has been a problem throughout the history of the comic strip, particularly in comic books. It seems that the script has always taken a back seat to the art. Perhaps this is because the script is the one 'invisible' component of any comic strip. Anyone can tell at a glance whether a comic strip is well drawn or not, but to discern whether the script is any good takes a good deal more skill. The truth is very few people know a good story when they see one—other than the audiences! Many people in the comics business simply cannot tell the difference between a good script and a bad one. There is no answer to this problem, except to point out that, without exception, *the script is the single most important component of a comic strip.* Readers will tolerate barely competent art and scruffy lettering, but nothing sends a comic strip to well deserved oblivion faster than a poor storyline."

No writer is going to produce a work of merit every time he cracks his knuckles over the keyboard. Nobody is perfect. Even William Shakespeare and Charles Dickens wrote clunkers. Nevertheless a writer should always give every story he writes his best effort. Successful writers write with zest, gusto, love, and fun. If you don't then even your best stories will only be hackwork.[1] The early history of comic books is littered with the bones of men and women who cranked out stories in a mad dash to earn skimpy paychecks

How skimpy?

Stan Lee, co-creator of Spider-Man, The Fantastic Four, and other landmark superheroes recalls in *Origin of Marvel Comics* (1974), "If memory serves me (and why shouldn't it?), I think I received about fifty cents per page for a script I wrote in those early days." It is small wonder that the stories written under these conditions resulted in the term "comic book story" becoming an Americanism for trash literature, but there were some outstanding comics stories written during this time by extremely talented writers like Eisner, Kurtzman, Bill Gaines, Jack Cole, and Bill Finger. Unfortunately their work is often overlooked and therefore ignored by people who might enjoy discovering them simply because they are comic book stories.

> *If you are writing without zest, without gusto, without love, without fun, you are only half a writer. It means you are so busy keeping one eye on the commercial market, or one ear peeled for the avant-garde coterie, that you are not being yourself. You don't even know yourself.*
> *- Ray Bradbury*

---

[1] During a *Comics Journal* interview with writer Steve Gerber (*Man-Thing, Omega The Unknown*), editor Gary Groth mentioned to Gerber that fellow comic book writer "Denny O'Neil once told me that 20% of his scripts he's proud of, 50% fall into the level of mediocrity, and 20% he does not want to think about." Gerber confessed, "It's probably like that for me, too. I've written a lot of tripe. So has everybody. I'm not excusing it ("An Interview with Steve Gerber," *Comics Journal #41,* pg. 44)." Along these same lines Chris Claremont (*X-Men*) adds, "Comics is a kind of artform—once you stop enjoying it and start hacking it out, the difference is quite apparent ("Chris Claremont," *Comics Journal #50,* pg. 69)."

6) THE BASIC ELEMENTS OF STORY

Riddle me this: is this following famous tidbit attributed to Thomas Baily Aldrich a story?

> "A woman sits alone in her house. She knows she is the last person alive on earth. Suddenly, there is a knock on the door."

Before I give you my answer, let us imbibe in a brief sidebar.

Since comics writing is a form of communication it is as capable of communicating any kind of material—be it fiction or nonfiction—as any other print or verbal-visual medium. During World War II, the U.S. military published a number of its training manuals in comic book format, and during the 1950s and 1960s corporations such as General Motors and U.S. Steel did the same with many of their instructional manuals. However, the average comic book buyer has historically purchased comic books to be entertained, not educated, and this is why most comics writing is creative writing.

Creative writers write **fiction** and *Webster's New World Dictionary* defines fiction as "any literary work portraying imaginary characters," a definition that dovetails with a statement Eisner once made that "Comics is a *literary* form that employs images [my emphasis]." If *Webster's* and Eisner are correct, then comics stories are **literature**, which *Webster's* defines as "all writings in prose or verse, esp. those of an imaginative or critical character, without regard to their excellence: often distinguished from scientific writing, news reporting, etc."

The Six Basic Elements of Story

According to the Greek philosopher Aristotle, a story must have a **beginning, middle**, and **end**. Since Aristotle's day trial-and-error has established that **setting, characters**, and **plot** are also basic elements of a story. With this in mind, let us return to Aldrich's last woman on Earth.

Does this tidbit contain the six basic elements of story: a beginning, middle, end, setting, characters, and plot?

The answer is ... yes.

There is a beginning (a woman sits alone in her house), middle (she knows she is the last person alive on earth), and end (there is a knock on the door). The ending is inconclusive, but—much like the 19th-century tale about "The Lady or the Tiger"—it is an ending designed to confound you. More than that, it is an ending whose intent is to give you a shiver, and in three little sentences it does just that. This story also contains a setting (the woman's house after some kind of mass exodus or apocalypse), characters (the woman and her visitor), and plot (the last person alive on earth hears a knock at her door).

For the sake of thoroughness, I should point out that some writers might argue that this tidbit does not qualify as a story because it contains no dialogue. I disagree. Dialogue is an important story element, one you will have to master to be a successful comics writer, but dialogue is not essential to telling a story. Even a comics story can be effectively told strictly through narration. This fact aside, though, a writer will have a much easier time selling a story if it includes dialogue since it is an element modern readers not only appreciate but expect.

Aldrich's tidbit is a story, albeit a rudimentary story. Not because it is so brief, but because, at its end, we know next to nothing about the woman or her world, how she came to be the last woman alive, or what affect hearing the knock on the door will have on her. A solid story does not simply tell something, it is about something. Aldrich's tidbit is a rudimentary story because it is all about scaring the reader by leaving the reader wondering who ... or what ... is knocking, an exercise bestselling author Stephen King (who knows a thing or two about horror and suspense) describes as using "imagination purely as a tool in the art and science of scaring the crap out of people." Rudimentary stories have their place, but no writer becomes a success only writing rudimentary stories. Successful writers write a complete story. To do that, you need to start with an idea.

7) THE JOY OF IDEAS,
OR WHERE TO FIND THE LIGHT BULBS

All creative writing begins with an idea about a character or a situation.

An idea hits you that worries in your brain until you concoct appropriate situations and characters to express it. Or your imagination is seized by characters or by situations that you cannot stop mulling over until their general importance become at least partly clear to you.

But where do you get ideas?

It is a logical question. It is also the question that is asked most often to professional creative writers. For what it is worth, I cast my vote with ancient writers like Homer that the source for all ideas is our Creator. That may not sound like very useful information if you are an agnostic or an atheist, but on the other hand if you do believe in a Higher Power that does not mean you should simply sit around waiting for divine inspiration to strike. It is nice when that happens, but like the saying goes, "God helps those who help themselves." If you subtract the Divine from divine inspiration you are left with inspiration, and I believe that the inspiration for all the ideas that you will ever have comes from inside of you. Inside each and every person is a stockroom of personal experiences shared by every human being. These common experiences become the grist for original stories when they are filtered through a writer's personal point of view—or what I like to call the **bent of the imagination**—because everyone possesses his own unique perspective on life. (We will examine the bent of the imagination in more detail in a moment.)

Everybody has been a child, has grown up, fallen in love, fallen out of love Everybody has experienced self-pity, self-approval, the anguish of loss by death, the slower anguish of loss by disillusionment. These are the things which make stories. These are the things which make them whether the stories are laid in Turkestan or New Jersey. It is not lack of experience which handicaps any writer. What it is, is the purblindness which prevents his seeing, or his seeing into, the experiences he has had.
- Edith Mirrieless

Reading Helps, but Not as Much as Imagination

Nothing spurs inspiration like reading, because reading is one of the best ways to find the **facts** that can inspire ideas. Edith Mirrieless, one of the great creative writing teachers of the 20th Century, calls facts "the springboard of the imagination." Big facts. Little facts. Exotic or familiar facts. It does not matter. Mirrieless insists that facts are "a writer's most necessary possession—

his most necessary except one, and that is the inflammable imagination to which the fact applies the spark." That "spark" is an idea, a story's moment of conception. The bad news is that everybody has an imagination, but not everybody has the kind of inquisitive creative imagination that can see the extraordinary potential concealed in the most ordinary of facts and ask "What if...?". If you have such an imagination consider yourself blessed, because there is nothing you can do to develop one. To paraphrase a popular sports cliché about speed, you can't teach imagination. "Facts can be acquired," writes Mirrieless. "Imagination, however, is mostly a gift of God."

Have you ever read a single issue of "Geriatrics, the Official Journal of the American Geriatrics Society," a magazine devoted to "research and clinical study of the diseases and processes of the aged and aging"? Or read, or even seen, a copy of "What's New," a magazine published by the Abbot Laboratories in North Chicago, containing articles such as "Tubocurarine for Desarean Section" or "Phenurone in Epilepsy," but also utilizing poems by William Carlos Williams, Archibald Macleish, stories by Clifton Fadiman and Leo Rosten; covers and interior illustrations by John Groth, Aaron Bohrod, William Sharp, Russell Cowles? Absurd? Perhaps. But ideas lie everywhere.
- Ray Bradbury

Developing Ideas into a Plot

The process of getting ideas is a balancing act. The writer has to look inside himself because all people experience life's joys and tragedies and these common experiences are the fodder for stories; at the same time, the writer must also look outside himself to learn about the world and to study the people around him.

But what do you do with an idea after you get one?

You need to develop it into a **plot**.

We will explore plots in detail in Chapter 9, but for now let me just say that a plot is the skeleton of your story. A plot supports everything in your story the same way that the bones inside your body prevents your body you from collapsing into an icky amorphous pile of yuck in your chair. A plot also drives your story ... propels your story ... gives your story's events the feeling that they are heading somewhere. Finally, plot is the method of transportation your characters use to travel from the beginning to the middle to the end of a story.

Ask Yourself Questions

The best way to begin developing an idea into a plot is to ask yourself questions. To demonstrate, let us return to Aldrich's tidbit about the last woman on Earth, a story so rudimentary that it could pass for an idea.

What questions does this particular tidbit spark in your mind? Some of the questions that come to me are:

- **Who is this woman?**
- **What is her name?**
- **How old is she?**
- **Did she have a family, and if so, what happened to them?**
- **What did she do with her life before this moment?**
- **Why is she alone in the world?**
- **What proves she is the last person alive?**
- **What the heck happened to everyone else?**

How many questions should you ask yourself?

As many as you need until you feel you have enough information in your head to write your story.

Remember that there are no right or wrong questions or answers for this idea or any idea. Writers are people and no two people are exactly alike. My experiences and the particular facts I have learned during my life are unique, unlike anyone else who ever lived, is alive today, or will ever be born, and the same is true for you. My personal storeroom of experiences and the facts I have learned will influence what questions I ask myself and how I answer them, just like your unique experiences and facts will influence what questions you ask yourself and how you answer them. These answers will form the plot that only you or I can write. Like bestselling author Ray Bradbury (*Something Wicked This Way Comes, The Martian Chronicles*) said, "There is only one type of story in the world. Your story."

Write What You Like or Don't Like

When you ask yourself questions your individual likes and dislikes are going to influence your answers. Most writers refer to this as their personal point of view, but I prefer to call it the bent of the imagination.

All writers write about experiences that are common to everyone, but everyone has an original perspective of these experiences because we each filter them through our own unique bent of the imagination. The reason everyone's bent of the imagination is unique is because different things interest different people, and original writing is influenced by the likes and dislikes you have that are strong enough to compel you to write about them. Since the things that interest me enough to spike my idea-radar may not even appear as a blip on yours, my point of view of a particular experience will be different from yours or anyone else's. Which brings us in a roundabout way to asking what seems to me to be the most obvious question about Thomas Baily Aldrich's story about the last woman on Earth: "Who's knocking?"

Could the knocker be something that slithers by starlight?
Sure.
Does it have to be a monster?
Nope.
A monster would be my first choice, but my bent of imagination has always been warped towards horror. I *love* monsters. Another person's bent might be spiritual, in which case he or she might envision an angel as the visitor. A science fiction writer might conjure an alien from another world or perhaps a time traveler from Earth's past, while a fantasist might imagine the woman's twin from a parallel dimension who has wiggled her way into ours.

However you or I decide to answer this question, a logical follow-up question would seem to be, "If the woman answers the door, what happens next?" After all, the identity of the visitor will affect the outcome of our story. If the visitor is a monster it may eat the woman, in which case the story is pretty much over. The angel may have come to comfort the woman, the alien or time traveler to question her, and the twin from the parallel dimension to aid her unfortunate counterpart. Notice, though, that whatever happens next depends on you. You have to decide who is knocking. It is your story.

Problems Can Be a Good Thing

This may not sound productive, but some of your answers are invariably going to lead to problems that you are going to have to solve as you develop your idea into a plot. For example, I would probably put a monster behind that door, but if I do that I am going to be confronted with a classic dilemma of the horror genre: **THE BIG BUG BEHIND THE DOOR**.

Nothing is so frightening as what may be behind a closed door, but nothing waiting behind the door is as frightening as what a person imagines is behind it *before* the door is opened. Open the door and tell the reader there is a ten-foot-tall bug, and the reader may tremble but he will also feel relief. "A ten-foot tall bug is pretty horrible, but I can deal with that. I was afraid whatever it was might be a *hundred* feet tall." Take it from a writer who knows, relief at the sight of an angel, an alien, a time traveler, or a twin from a parallel dimension is acceptable, but relief at the sight of a monster is a bummer.

More often than not **THE BIG BUG BEHIND THE DOOR** is a no-win situation, one some horror writers get around by not opening the door or having nothing there if the door is opened. Others open the door a crack so you never get a clear look at the bug. A few daring writers, like King and British author Clive Barker, prefer to throw the door open and let the chips fall where they may, aware that, as King puts it, "to open the door, in ninety-nine cases out of a hundred, is to destroy the unified, dreamlike effect of the best horror."

A prime example of the first stratagem is W.W. Jacobs' short story "The Monkey's Paw." So is Shirley Jackson's *The Haunting of Hill House*, a novel that never shows the bogeyman but supplies plenty of creeps by suggesting its presence.

Many stories by Arthur Machen ("The Great God Pan") and H. P. Lovecraft (*The Case of Charles Dexter Ward*) demonstrate the possibilities if you dare to open the door a crack. In these particular stories the monster is only seen out of the corner of the eye. A great example of this technique is the film *Alien* (1979) where director Ridley Scott does not give the audience a good look at his monster until near the end.

When it comes to opening the door all the way, creating a monster that does not destroy the "unified, dreamlike effect of the best horror" is difficult at best, but the rewards of striking pay dirt can be worth the risk. Richard Matheson's science-fiction/gothic classic *I Am Legend* is one success story, as are Lovecraft's "The Call of Cthulhu" and "The Colour Out of Space," but in my opinion the all-time best example can be found in the first eighty-odd pages of *Dracula*, where author Bram Stoker not only shows **THE BIG BUG BEHIND THE DOOR,** he traps the reader inside the monster's Transylvanian castle.

You are going to find yourself having to solve a whole lot of problems as you develop a story idea, but do not be discouraged because this honestly is a good thing. Solving problems will force you to (get ready for it) ask yourself *more* questions, and the more questions you ask yourself the better prepared you will be to write your story.

Bestselling author Clive Cussler recalls one day asking himself a "What if …?" question: "What if they raised the *Titanic*?" Cussler was immediately confronted with a logical problem: "The next question that entered my mind was why? Obviously the cost of salvaging the great liner from two and one-half miles down in the abysmal depths would be enormous. What reasons would justify the effort and expense." Solving this problem and answering other questions that popped into his head led Cussler into writing *Raise the Titanic!*, a landmark of the modern suspense-adventure genre and one of the first techno-thrillers. Cussler would never have written *Raise the Titanic!* if he had not asked himself questions and overcame the problems his questions brought to mind. As Cussler puts it, "Out of this pre-examination a plot was born."

When it comes to solving story problems, all any writer can do is rely on his experiences, his knowledge, his research, and his imagination. Your solutions may not be the best solutions in the world, but they will be the best solutions for your story, and that is all that really counts.

8) STRUCTURE,
OR THE SHAPE OF YOUR SKELETON

After you develop your idea into a plot, your story is going to need a **structure**.

Cussler calls structure "creative blueprinting," a solid analogy since *Webster's* defines a blueprint as "any exact or detailed plan or outline" usually but not always "of an architectural or engineering plan." A creative blueprint is the "plan" or "outline" of your plot. Put another way, structure is the shape of your story's skeleton.

As I mentioned earlier, a plot is your story's skeleton. This means that your plot is *everything* that happens in your story—*every* emotion your characters feel, *every* action that takes place, and *every* repercussion set into motion by those actions. In his landmark book *The Basic Patterns of Plot* William Foster-Harris calls plot "the map of the story," and all stories—rather they are rudimentary like the tale of the last woman on Earth or as complex as *War and Peace* and *Moby Dick*—have "a discernable plot form," a structure that is "the anatomy of story."

PART 1

A structure can be divided into three parts and contains the following three elements:

- **a problem**
- **a solution**
- **an answer**

If your story were a three-act play, PART 1 would be Act I. Your goals in PART 1 are to:
- **Hook the reader with the first sentence**
- **Get the action moving immediately in an interesting way**
- **Get your reader asking questions so he keeps reading**
- **Introduce your story's problem**

Readers want information in PART 1.

They are hungry for information.

Readers want to know about your story's time, setting, and characters, so you have to introduce all of these elements as you set your plot into motion.

But be careful!

It will be tempting to feed readers a cornucopia of data in PART 1, but it is never a good idea to overload a reader with information. Do not stuff your reader with names, places, and events. This can frustrate more than satisfy, so pace yourself. Reel out information only when that specific information is needed so the reader can follow your story.

The **problem** is introduced in PART 1, which takes up approximately the first third of your story. A story is all about characters accomplishing or failing to solve a problem—this is what English professors and creative writing teachers call **conflict**—so as you develop your structure you need to create traumatic moments that happen to your characters throughout your story. These traumatic moments are called **plot points**. As for the problem, a good tip to remember is that problems do not have to be represented by a villain. A problem can be impersonal (e.g., cancer, aging), philosophical ("To be or not to be"), or trivial (Ralphie wants a Red Ryder BB rifle for Christmas but Mom says no because he'll shoot his eye out). And attempts to solve a problem do not have to be serious or tragic. They can be funny, enlightening, thought provoking, or even controversial if you are feeling daring.

PART 2

PART 2 of a structure begins with the introduction of a story's first **complication**.

A complication is an unexpected difficulty that makes solving the problem even more complex. For example, having a character being coached over some sort of radio on how to diffuse a bomb is a classic problem in adventure stories. A complication for this problem could be that the character diffusing the bomb is instructed to cut the red wire but the character is colorblind.

In PART 1 of *Nightlinger #1* Mike Segretto's problem is figuring out why the man she is spying on (Nightlinger) is digging up a grave. When Nightlinger vanishes into a tunnel beneath the grave, Segretto pursues him. PART 2 begins when Segretto stumbles into the ancient subterranean metropolis. This metropolis is *Nightlinger #1*'s first complication. The metropolis is an unexpected difficulty that makes the problem of finding out why Nightlinger was digging up the grave more complex.

Most stories have more than one complication, and these complications build one on top of another until reaching a **solution** looks hopeless. Think of Indiana Jones doggedly risking his life again and again to keep the Ark of the Covenant from falling into the hands of the Nazis in *Raiders of the Lost Ark* (1981), or Chris Gardner nobly struggling against everything life can throw at him just to earn the slim

When your fiction's people think they have taken the right step, you must—for most of the course of the novel or other tale—prove them in error. As the story advances ... your protagonists encounter complications which seem to dash every hope, every valiant step. The worse things continue to look for the protagonist, the harder it is for him to find a way out, may happily stem from how difficult it is for you to discover an out!

- J.N. Williamson

opportunity to make a better living for him and his son in *The Pursuit of Happyness* (2006).

Beware the Trap of Act II!

PART 2 of a structure makes up the middle of a story, like Act II of a three-act play, and as any experienced writer can tell you this is where you will be at the greatest risk of losing control of your story. Like Cussler warns, "All too often a writer will sit down with a blockbuster concept and barrel through the first half of the story only to fall off a cliff because he had no idea where he was going in the first place."

You can avoid this trap by doing two things.

First, before you begin writing, make sure that you have asked yourself enough questions to provide yourself with an ample supply of plot points and then allocate some of the most exciting plot points for the middle. This will help keep your imagination inspired as you write, not to mention reinvigorate your reader just as his attention may have started to wander during this part of your story.

Second, create an ending for your story before you begin to write your story. Having this ending in mind gives you a destination to work towards when you get tired and your plot begins to wander or if you feel the temptation to pad your story. Odds are that situations will occur in your story as you are writing that will force you to change your original ending for the sake of story logic. That is okay. That will happen in creative writing. When it does, all you can do is replot your ending. This will mean more work for you, but your story will be all the better because of the extra time you invested in it[1]

PART 3

PART 3 is Act III or the end of your story. This is where you present the problem's **solution** (if there is one) and where you present the story's **answer**. The answer is the final reward or punishment that befalls your characters. The cowboy gets the girl or the Apaches get the cowboy. The villagers destroy the monster or the monster has the last laugh. The gangster falls in a hail of gunfire or escapes the clutches of Fate. The graybeard athlete hits one last homerun to win the big game or whiffs to wear the collar of loser for the rest of his days.

I think you get the idea.

A Good Structure Should be Invisible

The reader should never notice a story's structure. A good structure is like a good umpire at a baseball game: they are only successful if no one notices them.

A complicated structure can confuse readers by being too difficult to follow.

An awkward structure can distract readers by calling attention to itself.

And structures that suffer from a lack of originality can take the reader's mind off the story if the reader realizes that he can predict what is going to happen next in a story before the event occurs. Unoriginal structures are a notorious fault of soap operas, but as the popularity of soap operas prove there are times when a predictable structure is not only acceptable but expected. The term for these types of structures is **formula structures** and we will explore them later. Right now the time has come to take what we have learned about structure and take a closer look at plot.

---

[1] A tactic Oscar-winning screenwriter Stirling Silliphant (*In the Heat of the Night*, *The Poseidon Adventure*) used to avoid the Act II trap as well as force himself to create sufficient plot points was to begin writing a script with whatever plot point most excited him. When Silliphant finished that scene he would write the plot point he liked second best and so on, fixing plotting and characterization inconsistencies along the way until he had a completed first draft.

9) PLOT

According to McCrea the object of language is to convey thoughts and feelings from one mind to another without loss of *moving* power, and if a writer's style is adequate an idea will have free play and gain power to *move* in a reader's mind.

Stories require movement, too. A reader should never feel as if the events in a story have come to a halt. Those events should always feel as if they are heading somewhere, and the best way to give a story this kind of movement is to power it with the tightest, most interesting plot you can create.

Three Plot Types & the Dark Moment

In *The Basic Patterns of Plot* Foster-Harris categorizes three distinct types of plot:

- **the happy ending story**
- **the unhappy ending story**
- **the literary (or objective) story**

Along with these plot types Foster-Harris introduces the **dark moment**, the story's most essential plot point. The dark moment, which takes place before the story's answer is revealed, is where the main character decides how he is going to try to solve the story's problem.

Why is the dark moment so essential?

Because everything that takes place in PART 1 and PART 2 leads to this plot point. From the start of PART 1 the main character is moving (journeying) from one plot point to the next until he arrives at the dark moment; at the same time, all of the story's conflict funnels down to this decision, the most difficult choice your main character will make. Compounding this difficulty will be two conflicting emotions that will have waged war inside the main character's heart starting in PART 1. What these specific emotions are is up to the writer, but they must meet the following criteria:

- **One of these emotions must be right**
- **One of these emotions must be wrong**
- **The main character must be guided by one of these emotions to solve the problem**
- **The main character must not know how his decision will affect the story's answer (i.e., the main character is in the dark)**

This decision will instantly determine the main character's fate and the solution for the story.

The Happy Ending Story and the Unhappy Ending Story

As I mentioned at the beginning of this chapter, a story should never feel like its events have stopped moving forward, and one of the benefits of this is that the reader will always feel as if the event he is reading about in the story is happening in the *present*. It does not matter if the story is set in the past, the reader will feel as if the event he is reading about is happening *now* as the story moves towards the future, towards the dark moment, and towards the main character's decision.

In the happy ending story, when the main character reaches the dark moment, he will make his decision guided by the *right* emotion. If the main character does that he will make a morally correct choice and his fate will be a happy one and the story's solution will lead to (repeat after me) a happy ending

In the unhappy ending story the main character is guided by the *wrong* emotion and makes an immoral choice, so his fate will be unhappy and the story's solution will lead to (you guessed it) an unhappy ending.

To demonstrate let us take a look at Walt Disney's *Aladdin*, one of my favorite examples of a happy ending story. In this extremely theatrical and clever adaptation of "Aladdin's Lamp" from *The Book of One Thousand and One Nights*, the main character Aladdin gives his word to release the *djinn* Genie from a magical oil lamp with the last of three wishes Genie has bestowed upon Aladdin. As the film's dark moment draws near and Aladdin is forced to use his first two wishes, it appears more and more likely that Aladdin will go back on his word. Aladdin wants to marry his one true love, the Princess Jasmine, but Jasmine's father the Sultan has decreed that only a prince may marry his daughter and Aladdin is a lowly urchin or "street rat." Aladdin could marry Jasmine if he forgets his promise to Genie and uses his third wish to turn himself into a prince, but when the dark moment arrives Aladdin makes the morally correct choice and frees Genie. Aladdin appears to be sacrificing his own happiness when he does this, but Aladdin definitely does the honorable thing by keeping his word. What Aladdin cannot know when he makes this decision is that by keeping his word he will gain a sense of self-worth he has been missing throughout the story, and, even better, events will soon unfold that make it possible for Aladdin to marry Princess Jasmine.

A HAPPY ENDING. :-)

But what would have happened if Aladdin had made the immoral choice and not kept his word to free Genie?

Aladdin would have dishonored himself, so he would never have gained his missing self-worth. It is also likely he would have lost the respect of the woman he loves. Add those two things together and it appears Aladdin would have had a miserable life.

AN UNHAPPY ENDING. :-(

The difference between these two examples is the sacrifice that Aladdin chooses to make for the sake of someone else (Genie) and for the sake of his own principles (Aladdin's word of honor). "This is basic!" insists Foster-Harris. When the main character of a story finds himself at the threshold of the dark moment he must be willing to make a sacrifice like Aladdin's or the story will have an unhappy ending. Just as important, the main character must not know how his decision will affect his fate or the story's answer. This is why this essential plot point is called the dark moment: the main character *must* be blind to the future and has only his moral compass (his personal sense of right and wrong) to guide him while making his choice.

The dark moment can be tricky to understand since, in a happy ending story like *Aladdin*, the main character's sacrifice will appear to be heading the story towards an unhappy ending. On the other hand, in an unhappy ending story the character's decision not to make a sacrifice will appear to head the story to a happy ending. In both cases the result will be just the opposite.

Say the main character of an unhappy ending story is a father who has worked two jobs the past three years to save enough money to take his family on a dream vacation. This main character also has an older brother who has lost a job he has worked at all his life when his place of employment unexpectedly goes out of business. This brother needs to go back to school and learn new skills to compete in the 21st Century job market, but there is a problem: he does not have the savings to pay for tuition and to support his own family. The older brother needs to borrow money from his younger brother to make up the difference. Because this is an unhappy story, the younger brother refuses to help his older brother, *but* he is unable to enjoy the vacation with his family because his older brother will not be able to return to school.

Now let us take another look at a happy ending story. Common sense dictates that fighting a dangerous antagonist such as a Panzer tank patrol or a horde of mutant zombies can put a main character's safety at risk. Therefore, if the main character of your story would decide to flee the scene to save his life then a happy ending would seem to be the logical result. In reality, however, running away from a fight is the immoral choice. Fleeing will only make the main character feel like a coward (if the main character has any sense of pride or self-worth), and a coward is no good to anyone, especially himself. For this story to have a happy ending the main character must ignore common sense and fight the antagonist. Even if the main character is defeated the story will still have a happy ending because the main character made the moral choice. Even if the main character dies he will have died right like Mr. Spock in *Star Trek II: Wrath of Khan* (1982), D'Artagnan in the 1998 film adaptation of *The Man in the Iron Mask*, or Sherlock Holmes in Sir Arthur Conan Doyle's "The Final Problem," and that is also a happy ending.

The Literary Story

The plot of the literary or objective story moves, too, only it is in the opposite direction of the happy ending story or unhappy ending story. The literary story actually starts at the answer and moves *backward*, whereas the plot of the happy ending story and unhappy ending story moves forward as the main character moves towards the dark moment.

Sound confusing?

Hang on. It gets worse.

The main character of the happy ending story and unhappy ending story does not decide what his choice will be to try to solve the story's problem until near the end of PART 2, so the main character's actions can affect the future. This option is not open to the main character of the literary story. As Foster-Harris explains, it does not "matter what the main character tries to decide, tries to do, either course leads him to the same place—to the question of problem, where the [happy ending and unhappy ending] story begins." Because the main character of the literary story is powerless to affect the future, literary stories often end up being little more than explorations into human futility or misery, which can be powerful but also downright depressing if not frustrating.

To give you an example of what I am describing, let us look at a classic literary story.

Edgar Allan Poe's "The Tell-Tale Heart" features an anonymous main character, a madman, who narrates how he acted upon an impulse to kill a kind old man with whom he apparently shared a home. The narrator reports how he dismembered the old man's body and hid the parts under the old man's bedroom floor just before three police officers arrived to investigate a shriek that some neighbors heard coming from the house. The police searched the house but found nothing, so it appeared that the narrator would get away with murder … until he imagined that he could hear his victim's heart beating beneath the bedroom floor. The beating grew louder and louder until the narrator ripped up the floor and confessed to his crime.

Poe's main character has made a choice based upon two emotions, love and repulsion. The narrator admits that he loved the old man, but he became obsessed with the impulse to kill so he would no longer have to look at one of the old man's eyes, which was deformed. "The Tell-Tale Heart" is a literary story, though, so the narrator has decided to act upon his obsession and murder the old man before Poe's story begins. Because of that every event that happens in "The Tell-Tale Heart" is a result of this choice, and the story never stops looking backwards towards this decision as 1) the narrator meticulously plots, practices, executes, and covers up the old man's murder; 2) the police officers arrive in response to the scream that came from the old man before the narrator killed him; and 3) the narrator's conscience convinces him that he is hearing the old man's tell-tale heart.

Instead of starting with a problem like a happy ending story or an unhappy ending story, "The Tell-Tale Heart" begins with the narrator explaining that he has decided to commit murder. Making a decision like this would take place near the end of a forward-looking story like *Aladdin*, most probably at the dark moment, but the literary story starts at the answer and proceeds from there. Since everything that happens in "The Tell-Tale Heart" is a result of an action (the decision to kill the old man) that took place before the story started, that action cannot be undone, so there is nothing the narrator can do but succumb to his guilt, confess his crime, and face his problem—backwards.

Which Plot Type is Best?

I know you have heard this before, but the best plot is whichever type of plot you want to write.

Writers should write what they like, so if you like writing happy ending stories or unhappy ending stories or literary stories then that is the best plot type for you.

For what it is worth many English professors and creative writing teachers believe that the literary story is superior to the happy ending story and unhappy ending story because literary stories often make the reader reconsider moral absolutes and philosophies.

I, on the other hand, prefer the happy ending story with an occasional detour into an unhappy ending story. I prefer to entertain readers, and while literary stories are good for many things entertainment is usually not one of them. I also prefer the inherent suspense in the forward-looking happy ending story and unhappy ending story: up until the dark moment the reader has no idea how the story is going to end. Finally, the happy ending story and the unhappy ending story are the two plot types used in most of the religious and heroic literature that has influenced me as a writer and a person.

I am not suggesting that the literary story has no merits. Far from it. When it comes to examining human fallacy the literary story has it all over the happy ending story and unhappy ending story. Greek tragedies are literary plots as are most of Shakespeare's best plays like *Hamlet, Macbeth,* and *King Lear*. All I am saying is that the idea of writing a literary story does not excite me so I avoid it, and if it does not excite you then my advice would be for you to avoid it, too.

Write what excites you, not what you think will be judged as great literature. Writing literary stories is fine if that is what you want to write, but it is not the benchmark of a successful writer no matter what the people Bradbury calls "the avant-garde coterie" think. The benchmark is being able to craft a tight and imaginative plot. As bestselling author Dean L. Koontz (*Whispers, Watchers*) writes, creating good plots is the "most demanding task that a [writer] must face … the supreme test of self-discipline, craftsmanship, and art."

10) CREATING CHARACTERS

Comics writing is script writing. So is writing for television and movies. And according to television writer and script editor Stewart Bronfeld:

> Creating stories and the characters in them is what script writing is really all about. The rest—the technology, the business, the timing and the luck—are also found in a thousand other activities of life. But when, in the matrix of a blank page, a story starts to emerge which never before existed, and characters are born and develop who never lived before that moment, something very special is happening. It is part craft, part art and (there's no other word) part magic.

Characters are the actors in your story and the reader needs to care about them because good characters, like a good first sentence, hook a reader's attention and get him reading and continue reading all the way through to its conclusion.

Which brings us to yet another example.

Author and columnist Florence King is a real person, but you could certainly call her a character. When political and baseball analyst George Will (*Men at Work: The Craft of Baseball*) wrote a column focusing on King, he had to hook his reader's interest in the person he was writing about, just like a fiction writer has to do in a story. Will accomplishes this by describing King as "a pistol-packing belletrist" whose "family arrived in Virginia in 1672." Will continues, "Even her book editor compares [King] to 'a rattler with an attitude,' and he actually likes her, which is not easy to do—she likes her privacy and is a good shot—and he swears she wouldn't hurt a piranha." The important thing here is that Will grabs the reader's attention by describing King's contradictory and forceful personality with vibrant phrases that get a reader wanting to learn more about her.

Give 'Em 3-D Characters

One-dimensional characters cannot hook a reader. Cliché characters or characters that behave in a predictable way cannot elicit the empathy necessary to attract reader's interest. To do that, you need to create three-dimensional characters that feel real. This does not mean that the reader has to like your characters, but he must be attracted to them enough to want to vicariously experience their thoughts, attitudes, and feelings throughout a story.

One advantage the comics writer has over strictly literary writers like novelists and short story writers is that comics *show* a new character when that character is introduced. The reader can *see* what that new character looks like right away, but the prose writer has to describe his protagonist, antagonist, and other characters' physical traits. The comics writer has the advantage because people respond more immediately to what they can see then to what they have to read.

Despite this advantage, comics writers never should overlook that comics is as much a literary medium as it is a visual one. People do respond more quickly to the visual, but character descriptions in comics can be as powerful as any image. Here is an excellent example by Alan Moore (*Watchmen, From Hell*) from his *Swamp Thing* story "Roots." Moore introduces the superheroes Hawkman, Superman, and The Flash using nothing but descriptions as the famous characters remain off-scene:

> There is a man with wings like a bird ... There is a man
> who can see across the planet and wring diamonds from
> its anthracite ... There is a man who moves so fast that
> his life is an endless gallery of statues ...

These majestic and iconic descriptions emphasize the incredible qualities of these larger-than-life superheroes to readers unfamiliar with these characters. Moore's descriptions may also reawaken an appreciation for these qualities in comic book readers who could have become numb to them after years of exposure to these characters. Best of all, though, these descriptions hook the reader.

Frank Miller performs the same feat with Captain America in his *Daredevil* story "Armageddon." Miller does this as Captain America hunts down fellow superhero Daredevil in the latter's secret identity of Matthew Murdock. Murdock (who is blind but whose four other senses are super-sensitive because of exposure to radiation) describes this chase in first person:

> "No man ever breathed like that – down the block – in the
> alley – no – there's his scent – he's moving – though
> you'd never know it from his heartbeat – so steady –
> there – ran past me – rattled a garbage can – a little
> sloppy but fast – faster than me – no good – he's got it all
> worked out – right around the corner – leaping – so
> easily – window still creaks with his weight – three
> hundred pounds, at least – his muscles lie about it – like
> hydraulic pumps they swing him up."

Four Common Character Mistakes

These are common mistakes made by most beginners you should avoid.

Do not let your characters be totally self-centered. I will not argue that a three-dimensional character whose life is in peril will be worried about his own skin, but for the sake of depth and a sense of reality he should also be worried about someone or something else other than himself.

Your characters may believe that failure is not an option, but failure is a necessity if your characters are going to seem real. The best laid plans of heroes and villains do not always work even in outlandish action movies like the *Die Hard*, *Under Siege*, and *Rambo* series. Setbacks are a part of life. Nobody is perfect. Also, if your characters never fail, then your story will never have any suspense. Characters should grow and develop during a story, and one way they can do that is by learning from their mistakes, just like mere mortals do in real life. Strong and interesting characters learn from their errors and apply what they learned to what they do next.

You characters must "exist" outside the events that take place during your story. Except for the possible exception of Nicholas Nicklesby, the life of a fictional character does not begin with the first word of a story. Three-dimensional characters have a job, a circle of friends and family, dreams, and ambitions. Their pasts are spotted with sins, guilts, tragedies, successes, joys, and a host of experiences that will affect the kind of person they are as well as the type of decisions they make and actions they take.

People are naturally more interested in people than they are in circumstances. What engages their attention is not so much the adventure as the adventurer, not the danger so much as how the people react to what is menacing them, not the surprise ending, but how the characters in the story are affected by, and respond to, the surprise.
— Stewart Bronfeld

Avoid cliché characters. I know I mentioned this earlier, but this advice merits repeating. Avoid the strong but silent cowboy, the altruistic doctor with a secret, the absent-minded brainiac, the perfect housewife with a yen for other men, and the rest of their brethren. These and other cliché characters can be tempting for new writers to use because they are like pre-assembled toys ready to come out the box to be played with, but do yourself a favor and make your characters original! Every person ever born is different and unique, and the same should be true for your characters. For instance, if your story demands a strong but silent cowboy, make him different by giving him have a cherished dream of following in his father's footsteps and becoming an eye doctor in his hometown when his days riding the open range are finished.

Character & Plot: A Winning Team

Readers are not only interested in conflict when they read a story. They are just as interested in how your characters respond to that conflict. As explained in Chapter 9, the events in your story must always be moving somewhere and the best way to give a story this kind of movement is to power it with the tightest and most interesting plot you can create. A good way to achieve this is to let the plot develop out of characterization.

As you are creating a story's structure, keep in mind that your characters should never just react to its plot points. Characters are not chessmen to be pushed from plot point to plot point. Trust me, if you have created three-dimensional characters, they will take on a life of their own in your imagination and begin *acting* more often than simply *reacting*. If your main character is surprised by a Panzer battalion or a horde of zombies, he may *react* by retreating from the enemy, but the well-drawn main character will stop his retreat and *act* as soon as he has figured out a way to make a stand against the tanks or monsters.

Bronfeld points out, "In the lives of most of us, very few important things happen for totally external reasons; what happens to most of us is often the result of what we do—and what we do is often the result of what we are." This is also true for characters in a story. If your characters *act* rather than *react* when confronted by a plot point, then the characters will not feel flat, especially if they act in a way that springs from their personalities. Such characters possess depth and reality. They will feel real and your reader will care about what happens to them.

Motivation

Motivation is the reason a character behaves the way he does.

Unless you are purposely attempting to create doubt about a character for the sake of mystery or suspense, you need to make it clear why a character behaves the way he does. If, for example, your main character runs from those Panzers or zombies and decides to keep right on running instead of making a stand, be certain that your reader knows why your main character is fleeing instead of fighting.

It is a good idea when writing to stop now and again to see if your characters are behaving in a consistent and plausible way throughout a story. A good diagnosis for this is to check your characters' motivation. In real life people do what they do for a reason, and characters should do what they do for a reason in a story, so occasionally step back and ask yourself, "Is that how that particular character would act in this particular circumstance?"' Another benefit of doing this, if your characters' motivations are consistent and plausible, then odds are your plot is consistent and plausible, too.

Contrast

I love contrast!

It is the very essence of conflict!

Since everyone is different, it is only logical that people are not going to see eye-to-eye on every subject. No matter the relationship between your characters—parents and children, siblings, best of friends, new acquaintances, complete strangers, bitter rivals, blood enemies—there must be obvious psychological and physical differences between them. *That* is contrast! The more difficult your story's problem is then the more obvious the contrasts between your characters will become and that in turn will increase the conflict.

This does not mean that your protagonist and antagonist have to be polar opposites. There is no reason they cannot both be brilliant students at an Ivy League university or highwaymen in 19th–century Australia. Individually, however, they must be molded from very different clay. Perhaps one of the students stutters or is attending university after serving traumatic combat time in the military, or one of the robbers was raised a Christian and is developing a guilty conscience from his wicked lifestyle. Opposites also do not have to attract in your story, but nothing sets off a protagonist and antagonist or spices up a relationship between two protagonists like contrast. The *Lethal Weapon* film series is a good example. Another is DC's *Man of Steel #3*, a story that takes advantage of the contrast between the archetypal superheroes Superman and Batman to complicate the story.

Environment

Good characters reflect their environment.

A private detective living in 1880 England is going to talk and behave differently than one living in 1920 San Francisco, and contemporary cowboys do not behave and speak the same way that their counterparts did a century ago. No one is a total product of his environment, but no one goes untouched by it, so pay careful attention to how your characters should be speaking and acting based upon their backgrounds. That goes for appearances, too. The way your characters dress reveal as much about them as how they physically look. A county power line repairman from Wichita, Kansas does not dress like a New York City firefighter and a California high school senior does not dress like an intern working for a congressman.

Scenery and props also tell your readers a lot about your characters, especially in a visual medium like comics where they can be seen rather then described. Take for instance Bela Lugosi's portrayal of Count Dracula in the famous scene from the 1931 Universal film *Dracula* where Dracula welcomes a solicitor named Renfield (Dwight Frye) to his castle. Lugosi's Dracula wears the evening clothes of a cultured European gentleman, but the Count's dilapidated Gothic abode suggests he is something other than what he appears. Myriad spider-webs add atmosphere to the scene while suggesting Dracula's underlying desire and motive to trap his guest in the castle. A candle Dracula is holding casts a feeble light inadequate to wipe away all of the shadows and mystery

If you are not familiar with the environment in which you have placed your characters, research it carefully ... If, for instance, you have chosen the Louisiana bayou country for your setting, you will have to know what particular effect this particular place has on its inhabitants. Time is part of environment, too, whether it is the later 1970s or the 1890s. Any period earlier than the last decade should be researched for customs, social mores and behavior, modes of dress, and so on. Be at home in the environment, because until the completion of your [story] your life will be spent there—at least during your working hours.
- Constance Nash & Virginia Oakey

from his face. Even the vampire's cape suggests bat wings. This appears to be a character pretending to be something he—or it—is not. (Observant readers might be asking, "What is Dracula's motivation for pretending?" Go watch the movie.)

In 1989 I adapted the novel *Dracula* into a four-issue comic book mini-series for Malibu Graphics. For that story, I decided that I wanted something more traditional and less formal for the Count's costume than Lugosi's eveningwear. As for the scene where Dracula welcomes the solicitor (here named Jonathan Harker) to his castle, I wanted it to be more in line with Bram Stoker's novel, so the surroundings are noble and decorous rather than creepy and dilapidated, and Dracula carries a lamp that supplies a friendly boundary within the confines of his castle's nocturnal gloom. Dracula even politely shakes his visitor's hand. Mindful of the Count's true nature, however, I asked the artist Robert Schneiders to draw Dracula without a shadow. I also requested that a black rose (a symbol of death) be stitched over the "heart" of the vampire's shirt. Unlike Lugosi's Dracula, the Dracula in my script is not pretending to be a European gentleman. This Dracula is a no-nonsense warrior-count who is confident his visitor will never realize the obvious until it is too late: that the Count is the king of the undead.

It is up to You

Characterization, like plot, boils down to one simple fact: *nothing happens in your story by accident.* Whether or not your characters hook a reader's empathy is entirely dependent upon you. If you do not work to create memorable characters then your reader will not care about them, and if a reader does not care about your characters then they have little if any reason to keep reading.

Characters are what you make them. For example I wanted the Vampire-King in Malibu Graphics' adaptation of Bram Stoker's classic to be the very model of an eastern European warrior noble, whereas Bela Lugosi is *the* sophisticated and seductive Count in a tuxedo and cape originated by Raymond Huntley for *Dracula: The Vampire Play.*

ART NOTES
Page 64 *Dracula #1*, art by Robert Schneiders & Craig Taillefer © 1989

11) A FEW WORDS ABOUT DIALOGUE

Not all writers agree that dialogue is a necessary story element, but most modern American readers expect dialogue in their novels, short stories, and comics. Even Foster-Harris, who does not rate dialogue as a necessary story element, is forced to admit that "dialogue itself is a vital anatomical part of nearly every story."

Dialogue is more than verbal communication between characters. During the course of an average story dialogue also sets the story's tone, advances plot, and reveals character.

Revealing character may be the task most new writers overlook when it comes to dialogue. A character reveals things about himself every time he opens his mouth, not just by what he says but by the way he speaks. As mentioned in Chapter 10, a character's vocabulary, favorite expressions, and slang are all dependent upon his history and upon the time and setting of your story. A character also reveals things about himself by how he speaks during certain events in a story. What things make your character laugh? Shout? Moan? Complain? Sigh? Finally, when a character does not speak is also important. A character can reveal a good deal about himself during the moments he chooses to remain silent.

"Did You Practice Your Dialogue Today?"

Chances are you are going to master plot and characterization before you do dialogue. I base this prediction upon my experience that new writers tend to enjoy working on plots and characters more than they do dialogue. The problem is that writing dialogue—and narrative, but more on that in a moment—is like driving a semi or simultaneously tapping different rhythms with both hands. It is a skill that can become second nature, but for most people it does not come naturally.

To put it bluntly, writing dialogue is tough.

It is so tough that you must not let yourself get discouraged if you do not write appropriate-sounding dialogue on your first attempts. Because you won't. Dialogue requires discipline and practice, but all too often new writers get frustrated, or worse, slip into denial. I have lost count of how many times I have had new writers rebuff criticism about their dialogue by insisting, "My characters speak the way real people speak."

Trust me, hombre, they don't.

Writers do not write dialogue that sounds the way real people speak. Writers write dialogue that *seems* real. John D. McDonald, creator of Travis Magee and a grandmaster of the mystery genre, put it nicely when he described good dialogue as having "the *ring* of exactness and truth," and one of my favorite examples of this appears in Gregory McDonald's *Fletch* (1974), a novel told almost completely through dialogue. The example in this particular exchange is so good that *Fletch's* publisher inserted a truncated version of it on the cover of the paperback edition, and it loses nothing in the trimming:

> "What's your name?"
> "Fletch."
> "What's your full name?"
> "Fletcher."
> "What's your first name?"
> "Irwin. Irwin Fletcher. People call me Fletch."
> "Irwin Fletcher, I have a proposition to make to you. I will give you a thousand dollars for just listening to it. If you decide to reject this proposition, you take the thousand dollars, go away, and never tell anyone we talked. Fair enough?"
> "Is it criminal? I mean, what you want me to do?"
> "Of course."
> "Fair enough. For a thousand bucks I can listen. What do you want me to do?"
> "I want you to murder me."
> Fletch said, "Sure."

Real people do not talk this way, and I am not just referring to the topic of conversation. Fletch and his anonymous companion are speaking too calmly, too precisely. In real life their conversation would be filled with impatient sighs, strained and pregnant pauses, maybe even terser comments. Nevertheless, McDonald's dialogue *sounds* real on the page. It reflects McDonald's breezy, sardonic style even as it sets the tone of the story, advances the plot, and reveals character. (Do not believe me? Go read *Fletch*. You will thank me if you do.)

The rebuff that "My characters speak the way real people speak" is a trap that can prevent you from improving your dialogue skills. Do not fall into it. Dull or inappropriate dialogue stands out like a red flag, indicating to readers that the writer is an amateur. A good way to avoid this trap is, again, to stop writing every now and then and take a step back. Read your story out loud and ask yourself, "Does this sound real?" Over time you will develop an ear as to what dialogue (and narrative) does and does not sound good.

You will have to practice writing dialogue long and hard before you find a style that has the ring of exactness and truth. Reading the works of other authors can be a big help here. It will not be easy, but if you have the talent and the determination, you will eventually succeed.

Oh, and Narrative...

In comic book stories narrative typically appears in caption boxes. A caption box separates the narrative from the image in a panel even as it makes the narrative an organic part of the panel's composition. In this way word and picture operate as one, the essence of cartoon communication.

Narrative, like dialogue, should seem real, or at the very least natural. Readers should never be aware that they are reading explanatory or informative information, and a good way to prevent this is to avoid author intrusion or repetitions.

Author intrusion is just what it sounds like. The narrative becomes so awkward that the reader finds himself thinking that he is reading a story rather then losing himself in the pleasure of reading. Or the author struggles too hard for a clever analogy that comes off sounding strained. Or worse of all, the writer interrupts the narrative to step on a soapbox.

As for **repetition**, *Webster's* defines the word as "the act of repeating; a doing or saying again, or again and again." Repetition for the sake of clarity can be an important writing tool, but repetition becomes tedious or obvious when it is overused. Comic book writers must also be vigilant not to become repetitious by telling the reader what is happening in a panel. Let us say you are writing narrative for a panel that shows The Batman planting a haymaker on The Joker's pasty chin. Unless you have a really really really good reason for doing so, it is not necessary to tell the reader something like: "The Batman rains one thunderous blow upon The Joker after another." This may sound like common sense, but it is a common mistake almost every beginning comics writer makes in his earliest scripts.

12) SOME TIPS OF THE TRADE

This part of the book concludes with some technical tips you might find useful that I have learned through experience and from other comics writers over the years. The sole purpose of these tips is to help you communicate a message that has meaning (your story) to a certain targeted audience (your reader).

Remember: Room is Limited

Never forget that *there is only so much room* on any comic book page. The average dimensions for a printed comic book page is six inches wide by nine inches high. That is not much room, so be careful you do not cram too many words into a panel or too many panels on a page. At the same time, do not be afraid to use the space that is available to you.

A guideline that helps me avoid trying to cram too much on a comic book page is to aim for an average of six panels on a page and an average of no more than 25 words in any panel. Again, that is not much room, so you have to practice communicating what you want to say in a comics story as economically and forcefully as possible. The good news is that comic book stories have a visual advantage over other literary works that I believe more than compensates for these space limitations.

Suppose you are writing an eight-page comic book story.

Simple mathematics will tell you that you will have approximately 48 panels and 1200 words to tell your story.

In comparison, a short story writer writing an eight-page prose story (with an average of 250 words on a manuscript page) would have approximately 2000 words to tell his story.

That gives the short story writer 800 more words to work with, but he is going to have to communicate any important visuals such as character descriptions and settings that you can show in a comics story, and those descriptions can easily swallow up most of those extra 800 words.

If you are writing a longer story, say 24 pages, then you will have approximately 144 panels and 3600 words, while the short story writer writing a 24-page prose story will have 6000 (or 2400 extra) words, a good percentage of which will get eaten up describing what you can show in a comics story.

When looked at from this perspective, a comics writer can actually communicate more in a comics story than a short story writer can in a comparably-paged prose story. (See Conclusion for more information and examples.)

If you take away nothing else from this tip, remember that the space limitation in comics writing is just that: a limitation. It does not have to be a disadvantage so long as you remember that no matter how many pages make up the length of your story, you are going to have a finite number of panels and words to work with, so be sure to carefully choose what appears in each panel of your story.

Starting & Ending Scenes

For the sake of reader clarity, try to *start your scenes in the first panel of a page* and *end your scenes in a page's last panel*. Also, if a new scene features a setting that has not appeared in the story before, I will start it with an establishing shot of that new setting. This establishing shot immediately grounds the reader as to where he is so he does not feel lost. I would also recommend for the sake of reader clarity that you *avoid complex layouts and fancy camera angles*, at least until you become comfortable with comics storytelling. There is a reason why Woodworking 101 students build bookshelves, not armoires, for their class project.

Good Ways to Practice Comics Writing

Try to adapt a scene from a film into a one or two-page comics script. It is not as easy as it sounds, especially if you do not cheat and rely on the film's camera angles in your script.

After you have adapted a few film scenes, try to adapt some scenes from a novel. This will be a bit trickier than adapting a scene from a film, and not just because you will no longer be working with a story from a visual medium. To make a scene from a novel fit into one or two comics pages you are going to have to pare that scene's actions and dialogue to their essence. If you get frustrated trying to get the scene to fit into one or two comics pages, *draw a layout of your scene in thumbnails* as if you were creating a Kurtzman-style script. Do not get fancy. Simple stick figures will do.

If you give these tips a try, I think you will be amazed at what you will uncover about comics writing, not to mention how much more quickly you will learn this information if you stick to writing alone.

Learn How They Make Movies

Yes, comics *is* a verbal-visual literary medium. Its pictures do not move. Its words must be read. However, if you keep this in mind, you can learn quite a bit about comics by studying film production, particularly scriptwriting and storyboards.

The movie scriptwriter, like the comics scriptwriter, breaks a scene down to its essence and presents it as quickly and entertainingly as possible. Then a storyboard artist must translate this script into a series of thumbnail sketches that resemble comic book panels. Storyboards allow the director and crew to "see" what the film will look like prior to actual filming.

Many books on film production and about famous film creators include samples of scripts and storyboards, and studying how expert storytellers like Alfred Hitchcock and Orson Welles break down and communicate their films is excellent practice to learning how to break down a comics scene.

You may also pick up some unexpected tips that you can *adapt* to comics that will be useful for you. For example, to maintain a brisk pace in movies, a scriptwriter will rarely write a scene that runs longer than three pages or the equivalent of three minutes of screen time. After I learned about this I tried to adapt this guideline to comics writing, and after trial and error I discovered that limiting most of my comics script's scenes to one page prevents my stories from bogging down, especially during that Terrible Act II.

Action/Reaction

Something else I learned while studying film production is that film, unlike comics, incorporates **action/reaction**. In action/reaction, an action will occur in the first shot and in the second shot a character or characters will react to what just happened.

Action/reaction makes cutting from one camera to the next in a movie less noticeable to the audience, but I discovered that action/reaction is unnecessary in comics because *something can happen on the left side of a panel and a reaction can take place on the right side of the same panel.*

For example, Captain America can be at the apex of throwing a punch on the left side of a panel—the moment when Cap's fist should be slamming into his adversary's face—while his opponent is already flying backwards on the right side of a panel.

Another example: Perry White can stand on the left side of a panel giving instructions to Lois Lane and Clark Kent; meanwhile, Lois can stand in the middle of the panel, leaning on Perry's desk and arguing her boss' decision; and finally Clark can be racing out the door to carry out his assignment.

Comics ain't Dodgeball, but You Still Have to Block

Blocking is a theater and film term that refers to where actors are positioned in a scene. Knowing how to block your characters in a panel is important, as is blocking where you place dialogue balloons and narrative captions. Because comics in Western countries are read from left to right, the first character to speak in a panel should appear on that panel's left side. If a panel begins with a caption, then place the caption on the left side of the panel. From here proceed to the right with the next character to speak or the next caption to appear.

When blocking a panel, consider who is going to initiate the panel's action. Think about how any other characters that appear in the panel may react to that action. Ask yourself if it would it be better if some explanatory narrative started the panel instead of dialogue. For example, a previous scene could end with The Batman escaping a death trap set by The Joker. The first panel of the following scene could begin with a caption that tells us, "News of The Batman's escape soon reaches The Joker's Ha-Hacienda," and we see The Joker bellowing in reaction to this information. You may just want to show The Joker in this panel. There is nothing wrong with that, but there is also nothing wrong with showing some of The Joker's henchmen cowering in fear elsewhere in the panel. It all depends on what will work best for your story.

The 180-Degree Rule

One helpful blocking tip for beginners is to keep the **180-degree rule** in mind. If you show two characters in a panel at the start of a scene, imagine drawing a line between these two characters that cuts the panel in half. For the sake of reader clarity, make sure that your camera does not cross that imaginary line for the remainder of this scene.

To borrow a film example, say you have two characters sitting in the front seat of a car. If the camera establishes this fact by looking through the car's front windshield, then for the remainder of that scene the camera should not cut to a view from the car's backseat. The camera will look in through the driver-side window or the passenger-side window, but it will not cut behind the two characters, lest the viewer suddenly becomes confused about who is sitting on the left and who is sitting on the right.

Formula Structures & the Pros and Cons of "Borrowing"

In Chapter Eight, I mentioned that there are times when a **formula structure** is not only acceptable but expected by readers. A formula structure typically comes from a story that has become so popular that its structure is frequently "borrowed" by other writers. Readers who enjoy a particular formula structure expect to recognize it as they are reading a story and would be disappointed if that formula was not followed, an attitude that explains the continuing popularity of soap operas.

Formula structures are most often associated with popular genres like western and adventure (which often follow a good-eventually-triumphs-over-evil formula) and slasher films (where evil will eventually triumph over sex-crazed teenagers). Formula structures can also become associated with a particular writer, character, or medium. In the 1960s Stan Lee hit upon a formula structure for his Marvel Comics stories that became *the* superhero story structure in comic books for the next several years:

> The material will be arranged in roughly the following way: a three-page fight or chase scene to open; about two pages of the character in his secret identity; three more pages of the character back in costume, either engaged in a second fight with the villain or swinging around the city looking for the villain and encountering other little obstacles along the way; a couple more pages of the alter ego; and then the big fight scene at the end.
> (-Steve Gerber breaking down Stan Lee's formula structure)

Original writing features original structures, but formula structures can be a useful tool for beginning writers, which is a good thing since most beginning writers instinctively borrow formula structures when writing their first stories. Many English professors and creative writing teachers tell their students not to do this, but I insist that *there is nothing wrong with beginning writers borrowing formula structures*. I will even go a step further. I insist that not only borrowing a formula structure but *a favorite author's style* is a completely good thing for a beginning writer to do.

All creative people imitate. Even prodigies. A young dancer begins learning his craft by mimicking a master like Fred Astaire, an actor James Cagney, a painter Pablo Picasso, a sculptor Auguste Rodin, a musician Charlie Parker, a singer Patsy Cline, a composer George Gershwin, a writer Dashiell Hammett, and a comics writer Will Eisner. Even Bradbury believes "imitation is natural and necessary to the beginning writer," because imitation is a natural learning aid. The goal of every writer is to be an original writer, but when I say "original" I mean the same thing as lawyer and judge Sir James Fitzjames Stephen when he wrote, "Originality does not consist in saying what no one has ever said before, but in saying exactly what you think yourself."

Imitation is fine. In this particular instance, I encourage it. Just do not forget that you never will be able to say exactly what you think so long as you pattern your writing after someone else's stories.

In the prepatory years, a writer must select that field where he thinks his ideas will develop comfortably. If his nature in any way resembles the Hemingway philosophy, it is correct that he will imitate Hemingway. If Lawrence is his hero, a period of imitating Lawrence will follow. If the westerns of Eugene Manlove Rhodes are an influence, it will show in the writer's work. Work and imitation go together in the process of learning. It is only when imitation outruns its natural function that a man prevents his becoming truly creative. Some writers will take years, some a few months, before they come upon the truly original story in themselves. After millions of words of imitation, when I was twenty-two years old I suddenly made the breakthrough, relaxed, that is, into originality with a "science-fiction" story that was entirely my "own."
- Ray Bradbury

Parting Words

I cannot think of a better way to conclude this chapter then with some practical advice on what it takes to write from two writers who paid the price and appreciated the sacrifice. First, Alan Rodgers (*Bone Music*, "The Boy Who Came Back From the Dead"):

> It takes a LONG time to learn to write. Most of the writers I deal with spent somewhere between ten and fifteen years learning to write and establishing themselves before their work even began to sell. At the World Science Fiction Convention this year [1986], I looked around and realized that all the hot young writers were at least thirty-five years old.

Up next is Alexandre Dumas, and all he ever did was write *The Three Musketeers* and *The Count of Monte Cristo*:

> From that moment my career was decided: I felt that the special call which is sent to every man had come to me, then; I felt a confidence which has never since failed me. Nevertheless I did not disguise from myself the difficulties which such a life-work would involve. I knew that above all other professions this one demanded deep and special study, and that, to operate with success upon living life, I should first need to study 'dead nature' long and earnestly. Shakespeare, Corneille, Moliere, Calderon, Goethe, and Schiller—I laid their works before me, like bodies on the surgeon's table, and with scalpel in hand, long nights through, I probed them to the heart to discover the secret of their life. I saw by what admirable mechanism these authors set the nerves and muscles of their creatures moving and working, and noted with what skill they clothed and re-clothed with different flesh that framework which was always the same.

PART 3: PUTTING IT ALL TOGETHER

13) SPRINGBOARDS, SYNOPSES, SCRIPTS & COMICS

Springboards

Writers typically pitch story ideas and series concepts to an editor or publisher in the form of a **springboard**, a very short description of your story or series, usually no longer than one or two sentences. Here are two springboard samples:

> TATTERS: A contemporary gothic-adventure about a masked mystery man trying to uncover his past while aiding the people who live in the ghetto around him.
>
> WOLVERSTONE AND DAVIS: A series that weds the superhero and police procedural genres. In the near future, superheroes must work with law enforcement if they want to use their powers.

A springboard must immediately hook an editor's or a publisher's attention. The goal with a springboard is to intrigue, not explain, a practice used for years in news teasers ("A famous celebrity dies. Details tonight at ten."), television program descriptions ("Fonzie ski-jumps over a shark."), and jokes ("Hey, did you hear the one about … ?") An effective springboard gets your foot in the door by making the editor or publisher want to know more. If you can do that, you are 75% of the way towards selling your story or series.

Synopses

If an editor or publisher likes your springboard, he will probably ask to see a synopsis.

Synopses are designed to be read in very little time, preferably less than a minute. A **story synopsis** summarizes the most important plot points and introduces the main characters, while a **series synopsis** summarizes the premise, concept, prospectus, and characters. It is also a good idea to include three or four springboards of potential stories. One to two pages is usually an ideal length but that can vary depending on a publisher's guidelines or if an editor gives you specific directions about submitting a synopsis.

On Pages 76-77 is an example of a story synopsis. This is one that I wrote for a western, *The Bushwhackers*, which was never accepted by a comic book publisher but was published as a hardcover novel by Avalon Books and a paperback by both Dorchester Publishing and AmazonEncore:

THE BUSHWHACKERS

NAME
ADDRESS
CITY, STATE, ZIP
TELEPHONE OR EMAIL

(1879): LINUS GRIMM wants to kill the bushwhackers who murdered his brother and nephew, but SHERIFF JEB MOSES wants Grimm to steer clear of the matter. Since 1876, 27 people have been murdered throughout Moses' jurisdiction by the "cross killers," so called because of the "X" they carve in their victims' chests, and Moses is determined to bring them to justice.

These are two resolute men spurred by past demons. Moses, a reformed outlaw, exculpates his crimes by keeping the peace in Alma, Colorado, while Grimm, a former Union scout, wanders the frontier to escape his Civil War nightmares. Now Grimm wants vengeance, even after his father, ALVIN, a Mexican War veteran, advises him, "Killing can't help the dead, and it won't help you. Home and family cured my ills, and we need you." But Grimm believes, "All I am is a tracker and a killer. It's the only way I know to help my family."

Grimm enlists the reluctant aid of his friend MUDEATER, a half-breed government scout, and they pick up the bushwhackers' trail after a prospector is killed in Hoosier Pass. As Moses and his deputy, SCOTT COLEMAN, ride out to arrest the scouts for interfering, a party of mine owners frustrated by the cross killings post a reward for the bushwhackers. Soon after, Grimm and Mudeater rescue a young Arapaho from vigilantes after the boy kills a buffalo runner in self-defense near Chinaman's Gulch. Moses and Coleman pick up Grimm's trail there, unaware that the bushwhackers follow. Coleman is killed in an ambush outside Fairplay, and after his funeral Grimm risks arrest to suggest to Moses that they join parties. "Muddy's gone. He doesn't want to end up with an X on his breastbone, which he says will happen to us if we don't bury our differences." Moses accedes, on condition they bring the bushwhackers to trial. Grimm grumbles, "Fine, so long as they're agreeable."

Continued

Grimm and Moses begin anew at Fairplay. Near Jefferson they interrupt another ambush before the bushwhackers can cover their tracks, giving Moses the opportunity to identify the leader from a singular footprint. "His name's PEDRO MENDOZA. He was a legend during my desperado days. Big as a grizzly and twice as mean. Hell of a shot, too. Hates white folk with a passion. Came north as a Mexican delegate to the joint New Mexico-Colorado legislature, if you can believe it. Mendoza's a real patriot when it comes to New Mexico, and he swore he'd get even with Colorado for taking too much New Mexico territory when we became a state in '76. These killings must be his way of doing that." Grimm and Moses track the bushwhackers to their hideout in Lost Park, a forested glen surrounded on three sides by cliffs and swamps. "No wonder you never found them," Grimm confesses to Moses. "This is the most primitive spot I've ever seen."

Grimm and Moses invade Lost Park at dawn. An attempt to surprise the bushwhackers fails and a gun battle ensues. Moses is killed during the shooting, as are Mendoza's four compatriots. When Mendoza tries to escape, Grimm pursues, and in a vicious fight Grimm subdues the big Mexican but doesn't kill him, conquering his own need for vengeance so he can stop running from his nightmares.

Series synopses are longer than story synopses, but it is a good idea to keep the page count to five pages. Less is better. I always aim for two pages because it is better to aim high and miss than not try at all, but sometimes you just have to do what you have to do. On pages 78-80 you will find an example of a three-page series synopsis that I wrote for David D. Arnold's nifty series *Mighty 1*:

NAME
ADDRESS
CITY, STATE, ZIP
EMAIL ADDRESS OR PHONE NUMBER

Mighty 1

Created by David Arnold
Synopsis by Steven Jones

"More than just a knock out."

When a beautiful young 5'2" woman decides to tackle the fashion world that is hardly news. When she cold-cocks a 50' monster rampaging through New York City on national TV, buddy, that *is* news.

Introducing Christina Puissant. But you can call her Mighty 1.

Premise

Christina is the founder and principal owner of *Mighty Threads*, fashion designer to the superhero set. (Where did you think they got those costumes?) She is also a human dynamo, maybe the strongest person on earth.

When Christina was born 22 years ago, her father, the renowned archaeologist Dr. Paul Puissant, was excavating a site inside a milefort along Hadrian's Wall in England. He discovered an exquisite egg-shaped ruby the size of a large piece of hail, perfectly smooth except for two small chips. Returning to France to see his new daughter, Dr. Puissant gave baby Christina a present that would change her life: two tiny custom earrings inlaid with the ruby's chips.

Months later researchers studying the ruby discovered that it possessed the peculiar ability to transform light into other forms of energy, and that its genetic matrix was unlike anything any geologist had ever seen, leading the researchers to suspect the ruby was synthetic, possibly extraterrestrial. This information was classified, so Dr. Puissant and his wife, model Alexandria Bijour-Puissant, never knew the potential risk to Christina.

By the time Christina was seven the earrings had grafted themselves to her lobes. Doctors assumed the graft was caused by some freak mutation on Christina's part, and the Puissants decided not to risk scarring Christina's ears by having the jewelry surgically removed.

By the time Christina was nine she was faster, stronger, and tougher than the healthiest boy her age. These attributes increased geometrically each year until Christina was superhuman, or, as her father liked to call her, "My little mighty one." Except for their closest family friends, the Puissants kept Christina's powers a secret. Christina was especially afraid that public knowledge would spoil her dream of becoming a model like her mother. However, by the time Christina was 18, it was obvious that not only her powers but her height had leveled off, and no matter how beautiful she was no agency would hire a 5'2" model. "Too short."

But Christine Puissant is no quitter.

Continued

NAME
ADDRESS
CITY, STATE, ZIP
EMAIL ADDRESS OR PHONE NUMBER

Instead of forfeiting her dream, Christina shifted its focus.

An excellent amateur fashion designer, Christina sweet-talked her uncle, Henri Puissant, into letting her open a design studio in an abandoned warehouse he owned across the Atlantic in the heart of New York City's garment district. Henri acquiesced, but despite Christina's best efforts *Mighty Threads* was going nowhere fast when, of all things, a team of superheroes called Alpha-Team-Omega approached her about submitting designs for their new costumes. A ray of hope! And then, while rushing to her meeting with Alpha-Team-Omega, Christina bumped into a 50' monster named Fafnir.

Concept

Christina's battle with Fafnir is the start of her somewhat reluctant superhero career. Although her heart is in the fashion world, events seem to conspire to draw her into one adventure after another.

Soon after the Fafnir fight, a rubber check from the unscrupulous manager of the female wrestlers Leather and Rawhide sends Christina into the ring during a televised bout to repossess the costumes she designed for the women.

Soon after that a gangster, Don Carlo Mastroni, tries putting the protection squeeze on *Mighty Threads*. Christina squeezes back, but does not count on falling in love with Don Carlo's son, Antonio.

Soon after that a homeless man seeking shelter from the worst storm in 20 years breaks into Mighty Threads and makes a bed out of a pile of remnants accidentally enchanted by a client. The remnants bond to the man, turning him into a Patchwork Man and giving him power over all forms of fabric. Blaming Mighty Threads for his condition, the Patchwork Man seeks vengeance against Christina.

Soon after that ... well, you get the idea.

Prospectus

Mighty 1 is an adventure series all ages can enjoy. Generally humorous, it also features moments of drama and pathos. But no anti-heroes. No "gritty" or "twisted" adventures. *Mighty 1* is a fun series about a likable heroine who has brains, beauty, a streak of confidence as wide as the Mississippi River, and the most impressive clean-and-jerk this side of the *Daily Planet*, but struggles like the rest of us to make her dreams come true.

Continued

Supporting Characters

Alexandria Bijour-Puissant

Christina's mother, retired fashion model, founder and C.E.O. of *Enchante* Cosmetics, and an international spokeswoman for U.N.I.C.E.F.

Janet Draisey

Retired fashion model, *Mighty Threads'* treasurer, graduate of the School of Hard Knocks of East St. Louis, and Christina's friend and surrogate big sister.

Ginnie Liabo

Mighty Threads' computer geek and graphics expert, Christina's surrogate little sister, and indefatigable bright-eyed optimist.

Antonio Mastroni

Wall Street attorney, son of gangster Don Carlo Mastroni, one good-looking stud, a pretty good egg, and the love of Christina's life.

Kristie Ann Owen

Vice-President of *Mighty Threads* and Christina's second mother and conscience.

Paul Puissant

Christina's father, renowned archaeologist, and possibly the wickedest golfer France has ever produced.

In the header of each page of your synopsis or any script you write you should include a place for your contact information: NAME, ADDRESS, PHONE NUMBER, and EMAIL. You should also include the story's or series' title and the page number. Editors and publishers expect to see this information on each page of a synopsis, so do not forget it! This information is used to contact you, plus it makes it quick and easy for the editor or publisher to reassemble a multi-page synopsis if the pages somehow become separated during the submission process.

Scripts

If your synopsis is accepted, the next step for you is to write a **script**. Starting on page 82 are the page descriptions from a **plot-script** for Pages 1-6 of *Talismen #1*, the first installment of a comic book adaptation of the young adult fantasy novel *Talismen: The Knightmare Knife*. Starting on page 83 are Pages 1-6 from the comic book story drawn and lettered by co-creator Barb Jacobs. (NOTE: Normally I include character descriptions when a character first appears in a script, but Jacobs designed all the *Talismen* characters so I did not bother to include them in this script.) Try to imagine as you read the page descriptions how you might have drawn this story if you had been the artist. You can even draw your own thumbnails. As you compare what you imagined or draw to Jacobs' pages ask yourself what are the differences in your narrative breakdown, layout, and composition from what Jacobs drew. Also look to see if Jacobs makes any changes in the narrative breakdown, layout, and composition in the script. If she did why do you think Jacobs made these changes?

PAGE ONE: Open with individual shots of our four boys—COLIN SINCLAIR, REGGIE SPENCER, OLLIE STEELE and TIMMY SHANNON—peacefully sleeping in their bedrooms. Last panel is an ESTABLISHING SHOT of the crystal towers of a dreamland capital, DUNCAN, rising out of its cloud. Circling around the towers is a dragon.

PAGE TWO: CUT TO the four boys awake and unexpectedly finding themselves standing in a Duncan courtyard. All four are dressed for bedtime (e.g., Reggie in expensive pajamas, Ollie more casual in a Cubs t-shirt and gray gym shorts). Ollie and Timmy stand close together, but otherwise the boys have some space between them. Timmy is confused and frightened. Ollie is confused and on the defensive. Reggie is confused but is pretty good at pretending to be calm. Colin doesn't give a fig who knows he is confused as he searches with his eyes for any familiar sites to tell him where he may be. Suddenly Timmy shifts gears into outright terror as he looks and points up as a shadow falls over them. "What's that?!" At the same instant a protective Ollie glares like a cornered wolverine at the OP Reggie and Colin, ready to rumble if either of them makes an unfriendly move.

PAGE THREE: In a FULL-PAGE SHOT we see a large green DRAGON attacking the crystal towers of Duncan. The dragon's wings are spread wide and flames percolate from its eyesockets as it blasts the tower's summit with its fiery brimstone breath, even as its tail whips out and knocks a hole in the next nearest tower to it.

PAGE FOUR: The boys scatter to escape the falling shards, but suddenly Colin forgets all about the danger and stops in his tracks when he hears an OP bell toll. He looks back and sees a girl, JENNIFER, standing under the courtyard's pentice, holding a candle-staff in one hand and an empty knife scabbard in the other, looking surprisingly calm as stone and other debris begins to fall down from the keep. In CAPTION we read, "As the dragon lays waste to the crystal city, the boy named Colin Sinclair spies the orange-haired girl…"

PAGE FIVE: CUT TO a FULL SHOT of Colin's tiny bedroom. It is night. A convenient alarm clock on Colin's nightstand shows that the time is 4:59. CAMERA concentrates on Colin, who has just sat up, startled by his nightmare. SHADOW, Colin's gray longhair cat, is curled up and sleeping at his feet on the bed, the boy's abrupt movement not disturbing the gray furball.

Colin throws off his covers—on Shadow—so he can throw his legs over the side of the bed and work up the courage to step on the floor. "A nightmare? But I never dream! Never!" Colin tentatively touches the floor with one toe, like a frightened swimmer at the water hole, and walks over to his window to look outside. Shadow, curious, hops down off the bed to follow. Colin wonders, "Why does everything suddenly seem different?"

CUT OUTSIDE for a shot of the Sinclair's small middleclass home. CAMERA is positioned across the street near a streetlight, the lamp in FG, and a man (PRATT with his back towards CAMERA so we can't see his face yet) is standing under its beam as he looks towards the Sinclair's house.

PAGE SIX: CUT BACK INSIDE Colin's bedroom as the boy bends down to pick up Shadow, the cat curling around one of Colin's legs. "Maybe this is how you feel after your first..."

CAMERA moves in for a MS. Colin stops just as he is about the take hold of Shadow, boy and cat looking at CAMERA when they hear on OP noise (a hound howling).

Colin and Shadow both dive for the bed as the OP hound continues to HOWWWWWWWWWL.

Colin pulls the covers up tight around his head and Shadow curls up at Colin's feet, hiding his face under his tail. "What's that?"

CUT OUTSIDE to the streetlight again. We can see Pratt's face this time as the man sternly but worriedly looks in the direction of the OP howling. In caption we read Colin's thoughts: "It sounded like a hound! Hunting! But that's daft! Hounds don't go hunting in Cardiff!"

Now let us take a look a **full-script** for a different story, *Street Heroes* #1, and see how artist S. Clarke Hawbaker (*Nomad, Samuree*) draws the artwork for pages 7-9. (FYI: To the best of my knowledge the letters are by Ned Poins.) Try to imagine like you did when reading the page descriptions for *Talismen #1* how you would draw this story if you were the artist, then compare what you come up with to what Hawbaker drew. Again do not just skim through this full-script and Hawbaker's pencil pages. Study them. Think about them. Ask yourself:

- **What similarities or differences are there between what you imagined and what Hawbaker drew?**
- **How closely did Hawbaker follow the script? Did he make any changes in the script's narrative breakdown and composition? If so, why do you think Hawbaker did this?**
- **How closely did you follow the script? Did you make any changes in the script's narrative breakdown and composition? If so, why did you do so?**
- **Is it easier to imagine layouts and compositions with a full-script or a plot-script?**
- **Which script style is easier to work with?**
- **Does either script style seem more restrictive?**
- **Do you think an artist comes closer to drawing what the writer wanted in the plot-script or the full-script?**

PAGE SEVEN:

Pnl 1: INT. NIGHT
UFOs' LOCKER ROOM. The detectives are removing things (clothes, mementos, odds and ends) from out of STASH and MOONEY'S lockers and packing them into separate cardboard boxes.

    CAP: THE LOOP, 2:02 am.

    #2: In the end, one cop's just as dead as the other.

Pnl 2: INT. NIGHT
CUT TO an ESTABLISHING SHOT of the efficient but under-furnished office of CAPTAIN MONA LEA HAACK. There are the usual awards, citations, photos, and commendations framed on the wall. A well-worn couch waits in one corner. There is a computer terminal with screen and a file cabinet in another corner. HAACK sits behind her desk reading reports.

    BLOOD (OP): Captain Haack?

Pnl 3: CLOSE-UP of HAACK looking up from her work.

    HAACK: Blood?

Pnl 4: FULL SHOT of a weary THOMAS JEFFERSON "BLOOD" DAVIS standing in the threshold of Haack's door. He is wearing a thick wool turtleneck, jeans, and a shoulder holster. In his hands he holds the two cardboard boxes his men were using in PANEL 2. Behind him we can see that business is brisk in the precinct. Officers and detectives are busy. Life goes on.

    BLOOD: Yep.

    HAACK (OP): Tactical Sergeant Davis, you look like crap.

    BLOOD: Come to think of it, my butt has been brushing over my tracks, sir.

PAGE EIGHT:

Pnl 1: 2-SHOT, MEDIUM SHOT
BLOOD deposits the boxes on HAACK'S desk.

    HAACK: How did it go?

    BLOOD: She cried.

    BLOOD #2: Here. We packed up Stash and Mooney's stuff, and I've
        dismissed my men for the rest of the shift.

Pnl 2: FULL SHOT
HAACK places reports in a file folder. BLOOD lies down on couch.

    HAACK: Fine. How are you taking it?

    BLOOD: I'll let you know as soon as my ears stop ringing.

    HAACK: Want a counselor?

    BLOOD: No. Thanks.

Pnl 3: 2-SHOT of BLOOD, tired, closes his eyes as HAACK puts file in cabinet.

    HAACK: You in the mood for some bad news?

    BLOOD: Uh-uh.

    HAACK: The brass has a dan in Room A waiting to meet you.

    BLOOD: Do I want to know why?

    HAACK: They want him in you Undercover Field Operatives Unit.

Pnl 4: FULL SHOT
BLOOD jumps off the couch, charging the desk. HAACK looks on sympathetically.

    BLOOD: Are they nuts?

    BLOOD #2:   The UFOs were organized so fancy dans wouldn't
        have to go into The Field.

Pnl 5: MEDIUM CLOSE-UP
HAACK holds up a directive from her superiors.

    HAACK: I know that, Thomas.

    HAACK #2: I also know the Chief thinks you were smart pulling your men
        back tonight.

    HAACK #3: He feels having a dan in your unit with FirePower loose in The
        Field is just as smart.

PAGE NINE:

Pnl 1: CLOSE-UP of BLOOD as he pleads his case.

    BLOOD: But FirePower isn't in The Field anymore!

    BLOOD #2: He's up north, riding shotgun over those munitions.

Pnl 2: 2-SHOT
HAACK stands up, handing BLOOD the directive.

    HAACK #2: That's my guess, too. I've dispatched an A.P.B. to the
           proper authorities.

    BLOOD: Then why send dans into The Filed where they don't
           belong?

    HAACK: Because I have my orders, and so do you.

Pnl 3: MEDIUM SHOT
BLOOD taking directive from OFF-PANEL HAACK.

    HAACK (OP): Now get down to Room A and make nice with
           your new disciple.

Let us end this chapter with one more comparison between script and comic pages, only this time we will look at a completed story.

The following script is for the eight-page *Mighty 1* story "Free Publicity" published in *Scales of the Dragon #1* by Sundragon Comics. The plot for this story was created by the series' creator and Sundragon publisher David D. Arnold. I adapted his plot into a plot-script, the script was penciled and inked by Christopher Jones, I then wrote dialogue and narrative for Jones' pages, and those pages were lettered by Sundragon's editor-in-chief John Olson.

Again, study these pages. Think about them. Imagine how you would draw this story. And ask yourself:

- **What similarities or differences are there between what you imagined and what Jones drew?**
- **How closely did Jones follow the script?**
- **Did Jones make any changes in the script's narrative breakdown and composition? If so, why do you think he did this?**
- **How closely did you follow the script?**
- **Did you make any changes in the script's narrative breakdown and composition? If so, why did you do so?**

PAGE ONE: An ESTABLISHING SHOT of Manhattan as seen from New York harbor on a dazzling mid-July morning. The familiar skyline spans the horizon in BACKGROUND as boats and ferries of various sizes and styles travel in and out of the harbor. "A warm and sunny summer morning in the Gotham of Manhattan," we read in CAPTION. "The start of another bustling work day."

Concentrate on a Liberty Island ferry chugging through the harbor. The water on one side of the ferry is churning and starting to buck with waves.

In the largest panel on page FAFNIR, a colossal batrachian-humanoid monster (e.g., Godzilla, Cthulhu, or an Empire-State-Building-sized Creature From the Black Lagoon) erupts from the water. FAFNIR towers over the ferry, the Statue of Liberty appearing in BACKGROUND to provide a scale of reference.

PAGE TWO: ESTABLISHING SHOT of the headquarters of MIGHTY THREADS, a renovated warehouse building somewhere in New York's garment district.

CUT INSIDE to CHRISTINA PUISSANT'S apartment. A digital radio alarm clock appears in FOREGROUND, showing the time at 8:32. A newscast is playing on the radio and we hear, "This is Tim Kelly, reporting live from WZON! The monster is leaving New York harbor!" CHRISTINA is not listening as she rushes around apartment, talking on her telephone in French ("I don't care, Andre! I need that material!") while picking inline roller skates off her bed. She has her back towards CAMERA so reader does not get a good look at her face.

CHRISTINA'S hands tug a skate on one of her feet as she speaks OFF-PANEL, "No! I need *titanium*, not titanium *blue*!" In English she adds, "Gawd, pay attention, why don't'cha?"

CHRISTINA'S hand slams the receiver into its cradle so hard she fuses the two pieces together and demolishes the table beneath.

We get our first good look at CHRISTINA'S face. Her expression is a mixture of horror and embarrassment. "*Sacrebleu!*" she says, but thinks, "Real swift, mighty one."

CHRISTINA grabs her oversized shoulder bag as she races out the door, oblivious to the fact her radio is still playing. "It's heading for the garment district!" Kelly reports. "Police are advising citizens there to evacuate!"

PAGE THREE: CHRISTINA blissfully skates down the street, listening to a Walkman, noticing people beginning to rush in the opposite direction from her but apparently not too concerned about it. "This is your day, Christina!" she thinks. "It took six months, but your studio finally got the nod to design the new outfits for America's premier super team!" Suddenly CHRISTINA notices the fleeing people. "Hey, why's everybody running away from me?"

PAGE FOUR: CHRISTINA skids to a halt as something OFF-PANEL commands her attention. CAMERA CUTS BEHIND CHRISTINA as she stops in front of a police barricade consisting of sawhorses, horseback officers, patrol cars, and uniformed beat cops. Coming up the middle of the street is FAFNIR, stomping on cars and leveling buildings as it leaves a wake of destruction in its path. (Where's Raymond Burr around when you really need him? "Well…it's big…and it's horrible!") Although terrified people are fleeing in all directions from FAFNIR, there should be no casualties in view. CHRISTINA is irritated as she watches this calamity, not yet noticing a BEAT COP rushing up towards the barricade, waving his arms to warn her away.

PAGE FIVE: CHRISTINA insists she must get through. "I have the meeting of my life in ten minutes!" BEAT COP tells her that the mayor has ordered F-15 Eagles to bomb FAFNIR back to the Stone Age in five minutes. "Yeah, right," CHRISTINA grouses. "Like I can wait that long."

BEAT COP has turned his back on OFF-PANEL CHRISTINA to watch FAFNIR, and is surprised when her hands reach into panel to dump her clothes into his arms. "Here," she orders, "hold these a sec'."

BEAT COP turns around in BG to see CHRISTINA speeding away in FOREGROUND, our heroine stripped down to her superhero costume. "Lady! What're'ya doin'?"

PAGE SIX: In a PAGE-WIDE, THIN PANEL whose top and side borders bleed off page, CHRISTINA races across page, leaving an awesome YAAAAAAAAA! behind her.

CHRISTINA rams into FAFNIR'S ankles, knocking the monster into the air like a bowling ball striking a 2 ¾ pound bowling pin.

FAFNIR crashes into the street, gouging a crater upon impact.

Watching and reporting all of this is TIM KELLY, a handsome reporter in his late 20s, broadcasting from a WZON microwave truck. He can't believe his eyes as he speaks into his microphone, "Someone's fighting the thing! It looks like a…a…"

KELLY'S expression changes from incredulity to wonder. "…girl! A beautiful girl!"

PAGE SEVEN: FAFNIR sits up, groggy, looking for whoever attacked it. "Who…dared…strike…Fafnir?" CHRISTINA skids to a stop nearby, dwarfed by FAFNIR. "Fafnir?" she thinks. "Oh well, just call me Siegfried."

FAFNIR cranes its neck to get a better look at CHRISTINA, who is waving her arms and acting like she is shouting.

FAFNIR leans closer as CHRISTINA continues her act. "Was…it…you? Speak…up!"

CHRISTINA punches FAFNIR, shattering fangs and almost knocking the creature's head clear around on its neck. "I said, 'You're making me late, pinhead!'"

PAGE EIGHT: In a large panel that takes up the top half of this page, KELLY, COPS, and any BYSTANDERS cheer and leap into the air as FAFNIR goes down for the count. (Little birdies or pagodas floating around FAFNIR'S heard, or cross-shaped eyes, are optional.)

CHRISTINA retrieves her clothes from BEAT COP, who mumbles, "Uh…thanks, ma'am."

"Yeah, yeah, yeah," she replies as she skates off. "Just tell the mayor if he wants my vote he better call off those planes!"

As she departs, KELLY shouts into his microphone, "The city's saved! It's over!"

At the bottom of the page appears a MEDIUM CLOSE-UP sketch of CHRISTINA inside a CIRCLE FRAME, the word "Fini" appearing in a banner panel beneath her. "Don't you hate mornings like this?" she asks the reader with a wink.

CONCLUSION

"He hadn't even the satisfaction of being unknown."
-Ruth Waterbury on Lon Chaney (1928)

So what is so great about writing comics?

In the film *The Princess Bride* (1987) the Dread Pirate Roberts tells an inquisitive adversary, "Get used to disappointment."

Disappointment is one of the most loyal companions any comics writer will ever know, visiting often in a variety of unpleasing forms: rejection letters, opportunities that crumble or evaporate, hard work that never returns your investment, or reckless high hopes dashed by "maybe" propositions that never receive a green light. If comics writing has taught me anything it is that the Dread Pirate Roberts was right, I should get used to disappointment, but it has also taught me never give in to it.

The biggest disappointment of my comics writing career was three years in the making, beginning in 1989 after the first issue of my adaptation of *Dracula* for Malibu Graphics sold out. That success got me to wonder, "If the adaptation of a classic novel can sell out one printing, imagine what the adaptation of a contemporary bestseller could do." So I wrote a letter to one of my favorite authors, Clive Cussler, to ask if he would allow me to pitch the concept of adapting his novels into comic books to Malibu Graphics.

I tactically decided to approach Cussler for two reasons. One, he writes adventures, a genre that translates well into the comics medium. Two, despite his novels' worldwide popularity, at that time they had only been adapted into other media twice, so any adaptations of them would be novelties to both comic book readers and Cussler's fans.

Cussler never wrote me back. Instead he telephoned to say, "I like it." Malibu Graphics liked it, too, and for a few weeks it appeared that my idea was going to become a reality.

That was when Old Man Disappointment decided to intervene.

Cussler's agent and Malibu Graphics could not agree on terms. Negotiations broke off. Cussler, however, gave me permission to approach other comic book publishers with my idea, and over the next three years I pitched the concept to every viable comics publisher in the United States. Most were not interested, and the few that were eventually changed their minds or stopped returning my phone calls without explanation.

Disappointing?

Sure.

On the plus side, though, if pitching Cussler's novels accomplished nothing else it did help spread my name throughout the comic book industry a little bit and publicity never hurts. Even better (to me anyway) was the opportunity I got to talk with one of my favorite authors.

Now, to be fair, I have experienced disappointment outside of comics writing. In 1996 author Ed Gorman (the Sam McCain series, *Sleeping Dogs*, *Trouble Man*) offered to put me and some other local writers in contact with a New York editor who was in need of dark suspense manuscripts. We all pitched ideas to this editor, and he asked us to write synopses and sample chapters for the ideas he liked. I mailed my submission package two weeks later, and by that time the editor had accepted submissions from two other local writers, so I felt confident that I had a book sale waiting for me just around the corner.

Then who should come a'calling but you-know-who.

The editor rejected my submission. "It's suspenseful, but not dark enough." There was a silver lining, though. The editor liked my writing and said he wanted to publish a book by me, so he asked if I had any more plot ideas. I did, and during the next year I submitted three more pre-approved synopses with accompanying sample chapters. The first two submissions were rejected and the editor never responded to the third. The last time I tried to follow up with him his assistant assured me, "He will get around to reading your submission soon."

Uh-huh.

Anyway, while comics writing has its disappointments, it also has benefits. For instance, from a technical standpoint comics writing can improve your prose writing skills, while from a business standpoint it can put you in contact with other writers as well as artists, editors, and publishers, providing the chance to create an invaluable network of peers.

How can comic book writing improve your prose writing skills?

Remember your Strunk & White? *The Elements of Style?* In that priceless text you will find composition principle #17: "Omit needless words." This is one of the best bits of advice one writer has ever passed on to another writer, and nothing can teach you how to omit needless words like comics writing.

In Chapter 12 I discussed space limitations and passed along the tip that a comic book page should contain no more than an average of six panels and a panel should contain no more than an average of 25 words. This means if you are writing a 21-page comics story you will have approximately 126 panels and 3,150 words to work with. On the other hand, a 21-page short story with an average of 250 words per manuscript page adds up to an average total of 5,250 words. Subtract 3,150 from 5,250 and you will see that a comic book writer has about 2,100 fewer words to tell his 21-page story than does a short story writer. The good news is that the short story writer has to describe things that the comics writer (who has the advantage of working in a verbal-*visual* medium) does not, but even so space is still a premium on a comics page, so learning to omit needless words is not just a principal, it is a necessity. As I will show below, learning how to omit needless words in comics writing can help you do the same in prose stories.

Jumping back a bit for just a moment to the topic of working in a verbal-visual medium, a common mistake beginning comics writers make is to describe something in their narrative that the reader can see in a panel. Let us suppose you are writing a comic book story where The Joker has abducted Robin and squirreled the Boy Hostage away in a deathtrap that will spring at midnight if The Batman cannot locate and free his little buddy. The Batman hunts down The Joker and, in one panel, you have the hero belting the villain in the chin. It does not make sense to write narrative that reads, "The Batman delivers a thunderous uppercut to The Joker's chin!" (FYI: 10 words.) Better to let the art show the action and include the bare minimum in narrative as well as dialogue. Perhaps something like this:

CAPTION:
11:58

BATMAN:
Where's Robin?

JOKER:
Hahaha—

SOUND EFFECT
(Batman hitting Joker):
CRACK

JOKER:
Ugh!

BATMAN:
Tell me!

(FYI: 8 words.) If you transpose this leaner approach to prose writing, you are well on your way not only to conquering principle #17 but also one of the golden rules of storytelling:

Show. Don't tell.

To demonstrate, suppose this fight scene was part of a short story. An inexperienced short story writer might compose something like:

> The Batman was angry enough to kill The Joker, but
> that wasn't his way. Instead he slugged the villain, nearly
> knocking The Joker's head off and cutting off a mocking
> laugh.
>   "Where is he?" The Batman yelled. "Tell me or I'll beat
> you to a pulp!" (FYI: 46 words)

The problem with this example is that it tells us more than it shows. It *tells* us that The Batman is angry, and it *tells* us that killing is not The Batman's way, and it *tells* us that The Batman slugged the Joker. If an experienced comics writer wrote this scene, it might read something like this:

> The Batman's fist struck so fast The Joker didn't have
> time to duck.
>   "Where's Robin? Tell me or I'll beat you to a pulp!"
> The Joker had started to laugh, but now he was almost
> too dizzy to stand. (FYI: 38 words)

Example number two is not going to win any awards, but it does show instead of tell. It *shows* The Batman hitting The Joker, and it *shows* The Batman demanding to know where Robin is, and it *shows* that The Joker is hurt. This example also leaves more for the reader's imagination to fill in, much the same way closure encourages a comics reader to imagine the action occurring between panels.

As for creating a network of peers, I cannot overemphasize how vital a resource this can be for any writer at any stage of his career. For example, in 1992 I pitched an idea to Caliber Comics' publisher Gary Reed of adapting some of H. P. Lovecraft's public domain stories into comics stories. Reed was interested, but only if I could get a different artist to draw each adaptation. So I contacted artists in my network and in a few hours I enlisted five volunteers and secured the deal with Caliber.

Do not forget that networking, like a river, flows two ways. Artists in my network have contacted me when they have needed help developing a story idea or writing a proposal. So have publishers that I have freelanced for who find themselves in need of a dependable writer. In 1995, Reed received permission to develop a Young Adult paperback line featuring Todd McFarland's popular *Spawn* as a tent-pole series. Reed was aware that I had written comics scripts featuring licensed properties for Malibu Graphics, and he knew that I was trying to break into the novel market, so he asked me to write the first two manuscripts of this new proposed *Spawn* line. McFarland unfortunately never approved Reed's line for publication, but I was paid quite well for my efforts, which is nothing to sneeze at when you have a family and a mortgage.

As you can see from this last example, networks are useful to all writers. When I learned that my first novel *King of Harlem* was going to be published in the spring of 2001, I contacted writers in my network for advice on self-promoting my book, on approaching distributors and retailers to stock copies, and on what I could to do to help retailers sell *King of Harlem*. One of my network friends was the editor of a respected mystery magazine and offered me a free ad. Another friend convinced me to join Murder Must Advertise, a cyber-site where mystery authors, retailers, and distributors swap tips on promoting mystery novels. I not only learned a lot reading the posts on MMA, I expanded my network of peers to include more novelists and several independent mystery booksellers.

This is not to say that I was a total novice when it came to self-promotion before I joined MMA. Far from it, thanks to my comics writing. When I was writing for Malibu and Caliber I had no choice but to learn about writing press releases, preparing press kits, arranging signings, and meeting editors and publishers at conventions because independent comic book publishers (i.e., any publisher who is not Marvel or DC) had to concentrate their small budgets on publishing comics. This left the task of promoting titles up to their creators, so I took a public relations course to learn about the business of publicity. I still rely on what I learned from that class to help me spread the news about my latest writing project to local and regional print and broadcast media, independent and chain bookstores, and comic book retail stores.

Did all my self-promotion work?

If you mean did all my self-promotion make me a big name in the comic book industry, the answer is no. I have my fans, but it is safe to say that most comic book readers have never heard of me.

If you mean did I sell a lot of comics and make a lot of money, the answer is still no. The most copies that any comic book I have written has ever sold is 24,000, and that was in 1989 when a top-10 comic book sold over 100,000 copies. I have never earned a whole lot of money writing comics, but I earn enough to make continuing worthwhile to me.

If you mean did I ever get the opportunity to write a recognized comic book like *Batman* or *Spider-Man* for DC or Marvel, then, again, I must tell you no. I did write one story for Marvel's *Night Man* comic, a job made possible by my network when a creative director I once worked with recommended me to a Marvel editor. Marvel paid me more money for that one *Night Man* script than I have received for writing any other script, but *Night Man* was cancelled before my story was published and, baring a miracle, no one will ever read it.

So, you might wonder, if I have never made a big name for myself in the comic book industry … if I have never sold many comic books … if I have never reached the equivalent of the major leagues in comic books … why do I keep writing comics?

Like I said in the introduction, I write comic book stories for the only reason you should write comic book stories: because I love to write and I love comics. To be honest, though, there is one other reason: comics writing is fun! I love seeing a story of mine come to life in art. I love collaborating with artists and editors. I love the challenges and advantages that this wonderful verbal-visual medium has to offer.

For the sake of full disclosure, I do have to add that there is one more potential benefit this medium offers that I have yet to mention. For whatever it is worth, writing comics can open more doors to the Hollywood entertainment media than any other medium. I know very few novelists who have had even one of their books optioned by a film or television studio, but I know very few comics writers who have not had at least one of their graphic novels optioned.

Did you see the movie *Men in Black*? It is based on a Malibu Graphics comic book mini-series that never sold more than 5,000 copies an issue. That did not stop Stephen Spielberg's Amblin Entertainment from paying a nice amount of money for the film rights.

Phil Hester, a wonderful writer-artist, co-created and wrote a comic book mini-series called *The Coffin* that never had an issue sell over 7,000 copies. That did not stop James Cameron's production company from optioning *The Coffin* as a television movie.

I, myself, have been approached twice about two of my comic books, *Nightlinger* and *Tatters*.

Why this interest from Hollywood in obscure comic books?

One reason is that most comic books are high concept. Their premises are interesting and can be promoted in 25 words or less. Another reason is that when you adapt a comic book for film or TV, half the initial pre-production work is already finished since the comic book provides you with a story and storyboards. Finally, since comic book stories are verbal-visual, they are usually better suited for motion pictures than prose stories.

So writing comics can have its disappointments, but it also has its benefits. If you dedicate yourself and keep your options open, interesting opportunities may come your way. I will not deny that Mr. Disappointment cannot also drop by if opportunities ever do come your way, but I can say that I have learned to be better prepared for disappointment in all areas of my life thanks to the disappointments I have weathered while writing comic books. That is a valuable lesson for any writer to learn. Maybe the most valuable lesson of all.

Addendum

Just to prove that sometimes good things do come to those who wait ... and wait ... and wait ...

Remember my story about the New York editor who never got back to me? One of the pre-approved synopsis and sample chapters I submitted was for a western called *Bushwhackers*. When I never heard back from the editor I filed the submission away, but around two years later I found out through my network that another New York publisher who specializes in hardcover books for libraries, Avalon Books, was looking for westerns, so I dusted off *Bushwhackers* and sent it out. Avalon liked what they read and asked me to finish the manuscript, but with the understanding that this request was not a guarantee they would accept it.

Long story short, I wrote the manuscript and Avalon did approve it.

Yea!

About two years after that Avalon contacted me to let me know they had sold the paperback rights for *Bushwhackers* to the New York publisher who had originally rejected it. I thought this was so funny I told Avalon, but Avalon was able to do me one better. When I mentioned who the editor was that rejected *Bushwhackers* I was told, "Oh. Well, the editor who did accept *Bushwhackers* is married to that first editor."

Funny how things work out sometimes, eh?

END STUFF

GLOSSARY

GRAPHIC ELEMENTS OF COMIC BOOK ART

COMICS: A medium, specifically a narrative told thorough a sequence of images with narration and dialogue included inside these images.

COMPOSITION: Images that appear within a comics panel.

LAYOUT: Arrangement of panels on a comics page or in a comics strip.

NARRATIVE BREAKDOWN: Division of a story into a sequence of comics panels.

STYLE: The way a writer uses words and the grammar of comics to tell a story or an artist handles pen or brush to draw a story.

IMPLEMENTS

SCRIPT: A tool used by writers to communicate a story to collaborators. Describes how each scene is to be broken down, and can include narration and/or characters' dialogue.

SPRINGBOARD (a.k.a. PITCH): A very brief description of a story or series, usually no more than one or two sentences in length.

SYNOPSIS: Summation of a story or series, usually no more than one or two pages in length.

COMICS SCRIPTWRITING TERMS

BALLOON: An area where dialogue appears. Often shaped like an oval with a tail pointing in the direction of character speaking.

CAPTION BOX (a.k.a. CAP): An area for narration or dialogue. Often shaped like a rectangle.

DOUBLE-PAGE SHOT (DPS): Two pages monopolized by one panel. Often used for panoramic scenes or for scenes with many characters and/or details (e.g., "DPS of dozens of Mongol warriors as they lay siege to a Persian fortress city").

FLASHBACK PANEL: Shows a moment that occurred in your story's past. FLASHBACK PANELS are usually indicated by thick borders and/or rounded corners.

FULL-PAGE SHOT (FPS): A page monopolized by one shot. Often used to emphasize a particularly important or complex shot, or to provide impact to the conclusion of scene or a story (e.g., "FPS of METALLUS dangling a battered and unconscious SPACE GHOST over the edge of a cliff and laughing manically").

GUTTERS: The space between panel borders. The most crucial implement of comics storytelling.

MELD SHOT: A shot where two separate scenes blend together (e.g., "MELD SHOT: SHERLOCK HOLMES' face appears in CU on left side of panel, but as panel progresses to the right it melds into a FLASHBACK of a London alleyway in 1880").

PANEL (a.k.a., FRAME): A static movie screen where individual events of a story appear.

PANEL BORDER: An outside edge of a panel.

PROGRESSIVE PANELS: A series of panels where a progressive series of actions proceed forward in time (e.g., "In PROGRESSIVE PANELS we watch as BATMAN charges the JOKER, leads with a punch, then kicks JOKER backwards").

ROW (a.k.a., TIER): A comics page is divided into ROWS where panels appear to lead the reader's eye across the page. The most basic comic book page is divided into three rows with two panels in each row for a total of six panels on a page.

CAMERA ANGLE DESCRIPTIONS: DISTANCE ANGLES

EXTREME CLOSE-UP (ECU): Emphasizes a very precise detail (e.g., an eye, a finger, a signature, a snowflake).

CLOSE-UP (CU): Emphasizes a detail (e.g., a head, hand, ball, or signpost).

MEDIUM CLOSE-UP (MCU): Shows a character from the shoulders up and includes some background detail. (Often used in television, where it is referred to as a CLOSE SHOT.) Should not be confused with CU.

MEDIUM SHOT (MS): Shows one or more persons, as in MEDIUM GROUP SHOT. The shot is usually waist high and up.

LONG SHOT (LS): The next shot after MEDIUM SHOT, it includes the entire body or bodies (in LONG GROUP SHOT) and more detail of the scene. Also used to reveal a wide area or a far distance.

EXTREME LONG SHOT (ELS): Encompasses considerable distance but without definition.

BACKGROUND (BG): The part of a shot that is or seems to be toward the back. Surroundings behind something and providing harmony or contrast. The surface against which something is seen.

FOREGROUND (FG): The part of a shot nearest or represented in perspective as nearest to the camera.

INTO VIEW: A character or object or setting that did not appear in a previous panel either suddenly or gradually appears.

CAMERA ANGLE DESCRIPTIONS: PERSPECTIVE ANGLES

2-SHOT: Two persons in a panel.

3-SHOT: Three persons in a panel.

ANGLE-DOWN SHOT: Camera looks DOWN at a scene from sky, ceiling, etc.

ANGLE-UP SHOT: Camera looks UP at a scene, from floor, ground, etc.

ESTABLISHING SHOT: A wide-angle shot used to establish the location for a scene in the mind of the reader.

OFF-PANEL (OP): Person, action, dialogue, etc. that occurs out of camera's view, but a character in the panel reacts to (e.g., "A shadow from an OP MONSTER falls across the unsuspecting BOB").

OVER-THE-SHOULDER SHOT: Camera looks over the shoulder of a character.

POINT-OF-VIEW SHOT (POV): Action occurring in panel is seen through the eyes of a character in the story. Used to transmit the character's emotions so reader can empathize. POV can also be used to show the point of view of the subject of the shot. For instance, the POV of a ship sailing on a stormy sea could be written:

Panel 1: POV SHOT as seen from the bow of the *United States*, a 19th century man-of-war, as it bounces over towering whitecaps on a stormy patch of the Pacific Ocean.

We know we are looking out at the raging Pacific from the viewpoint of the *United States* but not necessarily from the POV of a helmsman or anyone standing on the man-of-war's bow. The reader is made to feel he or she is a part of the ship, looking out at the churning turmoil.

PULL BACK: Camera pulls rapidly backward (e.g., "PULL BACK from DRACULA to show sun rising above the horizon").

REVERSE ANGLE (a.k.a. 180° CUT): The scene in this panel is 180° opposite of the one that preceded it. It alternates between two important subjects, such as two faces in a heated argument or an instant before a passionate kiss.

REVERSE POINT OF VIEW: The POV shot reversed to show the original subject (e.g., we see through the eyes of BOB as the MONSTER approaches).

SIDE-PERSPECTIVE: Camera looks at a particular character or an object from one of its profiles.

ZOOM: Camera pulls rapidly forward, enlarging the subject (e.g., "ZOOM in for an ECU of a matchbook lying on a table from previous panel").

PLEASE TURN PAGE
FOR APPENDIX

APPENDIX: COMPARISONS

In Chapter 3 I explained, "Unless a writer or artist is intentionally aping someone else's style, no two people draw or write exactly the same way." This is important to remember when writing comics, because if you know who is going to draw your story before you begin writing a script, then you can tailor the script to highlight that artist's strengths and downplay his weaknesses. This way your story comes out looking the best it can, which in turn makes you and the artist look your best.

Just to refresh your memory, in Chapter 3 I wrote, "If another writer and artist, say someone like Frank Miller, had written and drawn [Pages 1-4 of *Nightlinger* #1], he would not have used the same narrative breakdown, layout, and composition as [Aldin] Baroza and I. For example, Miller draws faces and anatomy differently than Baroza, so Nightlinger and Segretto would not look the same. At the same time, if Baroza had drawn one of Frank Miller's *Daredevil* stories, it would look fundamentally different."

Say the artist you are working with draws excellent characters but his backgrounds leave something to be desired (a common failing with younger comics artists). Your story has to have backgrounds, but it will look much better if your script does not incorporate too many settings that are difficult to draw. On the other hand, if your artist draws wonderful street scenes but his trees and rivers are less than spectacular, you would be wise to try to keep your story in the city and out of the wilderness (or any city parks for that matter). You will not always be able to make such accommodations for your artist in your script, but you definitely should when you can since your story will only benefit from it.

If you do not know who will be drawing your story before you begin writing your script, then obviously all bets are off. All you can do is write your script any way you see fit and hope for the best when it comes to the artist's abilities. Just remember that there is a good chance that whoever draws your story will draw some elements of it well and other elements of it not so well. I can also guarantee that whatever the artist draws will not look exactly like what you had in mind when you wrote your script. Both of these things are all right. In fact they are inevitable, since your style is going to be stronger and weaker in different areas then will the style of the artist who draws your story— something you should have already realized if you tried my suggestion in Chapter 11 about drawing thumbnails of my sample scripts and comparing them with what the actual artist drew.

In an attempt to drive this point home, let us see just how differently two artists can draw the same material. Starting on Page 134 is my script for Pages 22-23 of *Tatters* #1, an admittedly violent attempt to combine political intrigue with the superhero genre. The pencil samples accompanying the script were drawn by Jason Yungbluth (*MAD*). Beginning on page 138 are pages drawn and lettered by *Nightlinger* #1 artist Aldin Baroza. There are many differences in how these two artists drew this same scene, but to help you get started here are a couple of things you can look for:

- **Which artist follows the script closer?**
- **If either artist makes changes from the script, why do you think he made them?**
- **Does Yungbluth or Baroza emphasize character more than the other?**
- **Does Yungbluth or Baroza use backgrounds more than the other?**
- **Does Yungbluth or Baroza use light and shadows more than the other to help tell the story or create atmosphere?**
- **Does Yungbluth or Baroza leave more to the reader's imagination than the other artist?**
- **Does Yungbluth or Baroza have the easier layout to follow? Why?**

PAGE TWENTY-TWO:

Pnl 1: INT., DAY
FULL SHOT of gym/studio, where four more DECOY GANGBANGERS wearing ski masks (not counting the two on the stage) have arrived to simultaneously cover the cowed audience as well as make certain the CAMERAMEN and FLOOR MANAGER keep working so what is happening here will be broadcast. All four SECRET SERVICE AGENTS who had been guarding the gym's exits are dead. IMPORTANT: Somehow the drape over some graffiti on one wall has come down at least partially so we can see a healthy sample of an urban interpretation of the Ten Commandments. On stage D.G.#1 still holds DeWITT captive and D.G.#2 is still covering the wounded LYNN and SMABY.

    CAP #1: From here the plan is a cake walk.
    CAP #2: Kill DeWitt and any Secret Service grunts still breathing.
    CAP #3: Then sweep the audience to cover their escape.

Pnl 2: FULL SHOT of one of the DECOY GANGBANGERS (D.G.#3) standing in front of the wall with the spraypainted Ten Commandments, his attention centered on the audience and TV crew in front of him. He fails to notice that TATTERS is stepping out of a shadow behind him.

    CAP: Simple. Nothing can go wrong now.
    TATTERS (Whisper Balloon): Pssst

Pnl 3: POV SHOT
TATTERS' POV: CU of D.G.#3 who turns to look at us and falls prey to the OFF-PANEL TATTERS' mesmeric powers. Eerie light from TATTERS' eyes are reflected in D.G.#3'S eyes as well as the skin directly around his sockets.

    D.G.#3(small letters): UHHN!
    TATTERS (WB): Do like I say!

Pnl 4: FULL SHOT of stage as D.G.#1 talks with DeWitt while he and D.G.#2 (who has turned away from Secret Service agents LYNN and SMABY to look at D.G.#1) prepare to instigate the last stage of the assassination plan.

    D.G.#1: You were right, G. Ain't nobody safe these days!
    #2 (to D.G.#2): Whack 'em.
    D.G.#2: Done.

Pnl 5: 4-SHOT
D.G.#2 turns around to discover that TATTERS has appeared behind LYNN and SMABY, the hero startling the woman as D.G.#2 falls prey to TATTERS' mesmeric stare.

    D.G.#2(small letters): UHHN!
    TATTERS (WB): Do like I say!
    LYNN: It's you!

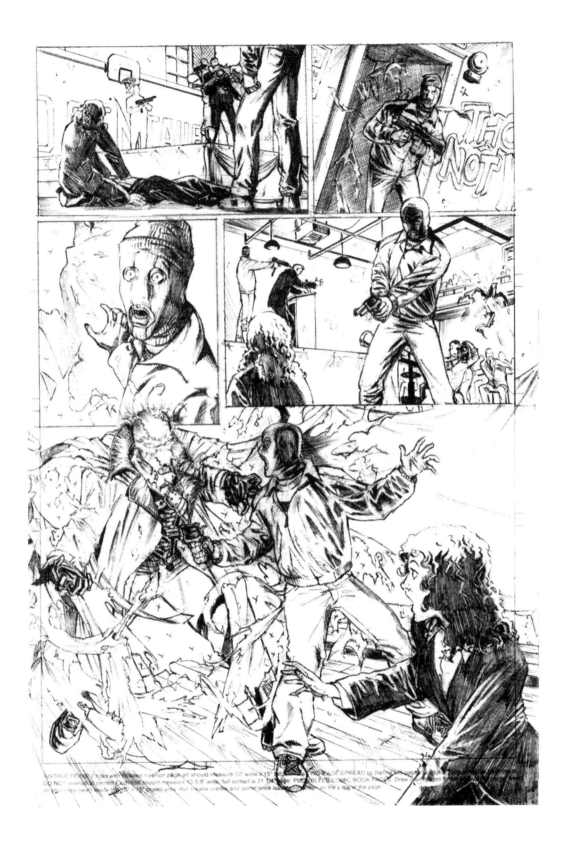

PAGE TWENTY-THREE:

Pnl 1: MEDIUM SHOT of the fourth DECOY GANGBANGER getting shot through the head by a bullet from OFF-PANEL D.G.#3.

    CAP (TATTERS): "Sorry. Can't talk now."
    SFX (OP gunfire): CRACK
    D.G.#4:   ***!

Pnl 2: MEDIUM SHOT of fifth DECOY GANGBANGER being taken down by another shot from the OP D.G.#3 a second after PANEL 4.

    D.G.#5: Hey--***!
    SFX (OP gunfire): CRACK

Pnl 3: MEDIUM SHOT of sixth DECOY GANGBANGER managing to fire his own round at OP D.G.#3 before becoming the third person in the gym to die in the last three seconds.

    D.G.#6: It's Lonni--***!
    SFX (OP gunfire): CRACK
    SFX (D.G.#6'S gunfire): K-BLAM

Pnl 4: THIN PANEL
FS of D.G.#3 being slammed into the wall behind him from the impact of D.G.#6'S bullet piercing his chest. This bullet ricochets off the wall, taking off a large hunk of the word NOT from YOU SHALL NOT KILL. Meanwhile D.G.#3 reflexively triggers on more round as he dies.

    D.G.#3: Guh--***!
    SFX(gunfire): CRACK
    SFX(ricochet): bu-tack

Pnl 5: FS
of stage as D.G.#2 takes aim and drills D.G.#1 through the left eye. DeWITT cringes in reflex. TATTERS is diving towards DeWITT. LYNN can only watch, frustrated and outraged to be helpless when she is needed most.

    D.G.#1: ***--!
    SFX(gunfire): BAM

    TATTERS: Don't move, Jeff!

Pnl 6: 2-SHOT
TATTERS grabs the terrified DeWITT even as the hero's cape wraps around the President like a Venus Flytrap.

    DeWITT: Keep away!
    TATTERS: I really think you'll be safer with me.

Pnl 7: SPECIAL EFFECT SHOT
PANEL becomes a television screen, on which we see LYNN (unable to stand) struggling to reach DeWITT as TATTERS disappears with the President. TATTERS leaves behind a temporary outline of his head and coat while his physical form implodes into a tiny electric dot that fades away.

    SFX (TATTERS disappearing): whoosh
    LYNN (EB/points to TV): Mr. President!

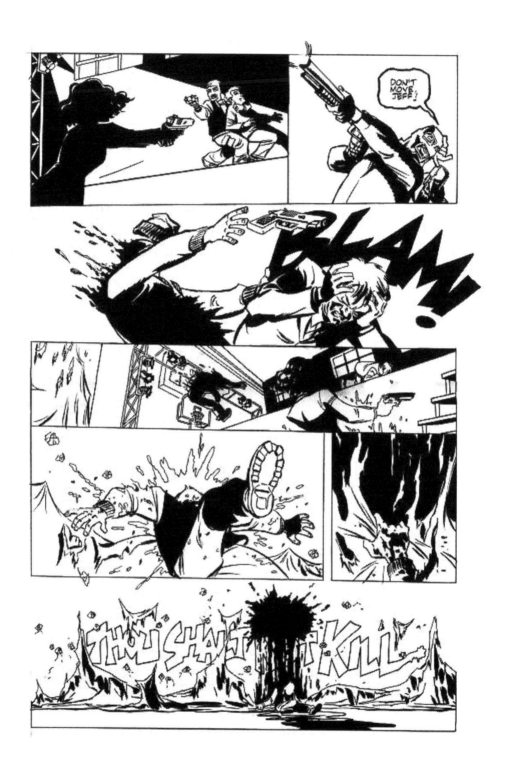

A FEW RECOMMENDED REFERENCE BOOKS

Comic Books

THE CARTOON: COMMUNICATION TO THE QUICK
Randall P. Harrison

HOW TO DRAW AND SELL COMIC STRIPS FOR NEWSPAPERS AND COMIC
BOOKS
Alan McKenzie

HOW TO DRAW COMICS THE MARVEL WAY!
Stan Lee and John Buscema

UNDERSTANDING COMICS
Scott McLoud

A WRITER'S GUIDE TO THE BUSINESS OF COMICS
Lauren Haines

Scriptwriting

PANEL ONE
Nat Gertler, Editor

SCREENPLAY
Syd Field

Writing

BASIC PATTERNS OF PLOT
William Foster-Harris

ELEMENTS OF STYLE
William Strunk, Jr. and E.B. White

IF YOU WANT TO WRITE
Brenda Ueland

THE WRITER'S HANDBOOK (1987 EDITION)
Sylvia K. Burack, Editor

ZEN AND THE ART OF WRITING
Ray Bradbury

REFERENCE SOURCES

Articles

Arnold, Andre D.
- "The Graphic Novel Silver Anniversary," TIME.COM,
http://www.time.com/time/columnist/arnold/article/0,9565,542579,00.html
- "Never Too Late: TIME.commix talks with industry legend Will Eisner,"
TIME.COM,
http://www.time.com/time/columnist/printout/0,8816,488263,00.htm

Barlas, Peter
"Stan Lee," www.angelfire.com/nm/Clutch888/stan.html

Beerbohm, Robert
"Comics Reality 11," http://members.aol.com/comicbknet/realty11.txt

David, Peter
"What Are Direct Sales?" COMICS SCENES #7, pp.49-54

Harvey, R.C.
"Comicopia," ROCKET'S BLAST COMICOLLECTOR #15, p. 58

Levitz, Paul
"A Call for Higher Criticism," COMICS JOURNAL No. 50, pp. 44-45

Luciano, Dale
"An Unapologetic and Eulogistic Critical Survey of Steve Gerber's Howard the
Duck," COMICS JOURNAL No. 63, pp. 152-162

Matheson, Whitney
- "Girls Get Their 'Shojo' Working in Comic Book Shops,"
http://www.usatoday.com/life/books/news/2004-05-12-manga-main_x.htm
- "What Animates Teens About Manga? The Stories,"
http://www.usatoday.com/life/books/news/2004-05-11-manga-inside_x.htm

Perkins, David
"A Definition of Caricature and Caricature Recognition," STUDIES IN VISUAL
COMMUNICATION 2, 1976, 1

Stallman, David
"Super-heroes: The Cult and the Fad (Including a Call for Radical Change at
Marvel and DC)," COMICS JOURNAL No. 57, pp. 107-113

Waterbury, Ruth
"Lon Chaney: The Man Behind the Monsters," FAMOUS MONSTERS OF
FILMLAND # 226, pp. 34-44

Books (Fiction)

Grell, Mike
Sable (Tor, 2000)

King, Stephen
Night Shift, "Introduction" by John D. MacDonald (Doubleday, 1978)

Lovecraft, H. P.
- *The Best of H. P. Lovecraft: Bloodcurdling Tales of Horror and the Macabre* (Del
Rey, 1982)
- *Reanimator Tales: The Grewsome Adventures of Herbert West & Supernatural
Horror in Literature* (Caliber, 2014)

McDonald, Gregory
Fletch (Avon Books, 1974)

Books (Nonfiction)

Benton, Mike
The Comic Book in America: An Illustrated History (Taylor Publishing, 1989)

Berlo, David K.
The Process of Communication, (New York: Holt, Rinehart and Winston, Inc.,
1960)

Bissette, Stephen R. & Wiater, Stanley,
Comic Book Rebels (Plume, 1993)

Bongco, Mila
*Reading Comics: Language, Culture, and the Concept of the Superhero in Comic
Books* (Garland Publishing, Inc., 2000)

Clute, John
Science Fiction: The Illustrated Encyclopedia (Dorling Kindersley, 1995)

De la Croix, Horst & Tansey, Richard G.
Gardner's Art Through the Ages (8TH Ed., Harcourt Brace Jovanovich)

Dembski, William A.
Intelligent Design: The Bridge Between Science & Theology (InterVarsity Press,
1999)

Eisner, Will
- *Comics & Sequential Art* (Poorhouse Press, 1985)
- *Graphic Storytelling & Visual Narrative* (Poorhouse Press, 1996)

Fleisher, Michael
The Encyclopedia of Superheroes: Volume I. Batman (Collier Books, 1976)

Harvey, R.C.
The Art of the Comic Book: An Aesthetic History (University of Mississippi, 1996)

Kane, Bob w/Andrae, Tom
Batman & Me (Eclipse Books, 1989)

King, Stephen
Danse Macabre (Everest House, 1981)

Klock, Geoff
How To Read Superhero Comics (Continuum, 2002)

Lee, Stan
Origins of Marvel Comics (Simon & Schuster, 1974)

Lovecraft, H. P.
"Supernatural Horror in Literature," *Dagon and Other Macabre Tales* (Arkham House, 1987)

McCloud, Scott
Understanding Comics (Tundra Publishing, 1993)

McKenzie, Alan
How To Draw and Sell Comic Strips (Quatro Publication, 1987)

Rawson, Daniel
Design (Prentice-Hall, Inc., 1987)

Schreiner, Dave
Kitchen Sink Press: The First 25 Years (Kitchen Sink Press, 1994)

Severin, Werner J. & Tankard Jr., James W.
*Communication Theories: Origins*Methods*Uses* (Hastings House, 1979)

Walker, Mort
Backstage At the Strips (Mason/Charter, 1975)
The Lexicon of Comicana (Museum of Cartoon Art, 1980)

Webster's New World Dictionary of the American Language (World Publishing Company, 2nd Edition, 1972)

Wells, H.G.
The Outline To History, (International Collectors Library, 1971)

Wright, Bradford W.
Comic Book Nation: The Transformation of Youth Culture in America (The Johns Hopkins University Press, 2001)

Yronwode, Catherine
Art of Will Eisner (Kitchen Sink Press, 1982)

Comics/Graphic Novels

Eisner, Will
The Dreamer (Kitchen Sink Press)

Grell, Mike
- *Jon Sable, Freelance* Vol. 1 Issues 1-5 (First Comics)
- *The Warlord,* v.1. 1-52, v.2 1-16 (DC Comics)

Miller, Frank & Mazzucchelli, David
Daredevil, Born Again (Marvel Comics)

Moore, Alan & Bissette, Stephen
Saga of the Swamp Thing (DC Comics)

Interviews

Gerber, Steve
"An Interview With Steve Gerber," COMICS JOURNAL #41, pp. 29-44

Grell, Mike
- "Mike Grell," COMICS INTERVIEW #69, pp. 22-44
- "Mike Grell, Freelance: Jon Sable's Creator On His Days of Independence," from COMIC BOOK ARTIST #8,
http://twomorrows.com.comicbooksartist/articles/08grell.html

Reed, Gary
"Interviews: Gary Reed Creator of Saint Germaine," JAZMA ONLINE,
http://www.jazmaonline.com/interviews/interviews.asp?intID=180

Shooter, Jim
"Pushing Marvel Into the '80s: An Interview with Jim Shooter," COMICS JOURNAL No. 60, pp. 56-83

Sim, Dave
"Dave & Deni Sim: A Talk With The Famous Aardvark Artist (And His Lovely Publisher, Too)," Part 1, COMICS JOURNAL No. 82, pp. 66-83 and Part 2, COMICS JOURNAL, No. 83, pp. 59-81

Staton, Joe
"From E-Man to Batman: Joe Staton Interview," COMICS JOURNAL # 45, pp. 37-45

Wein, Len
"Len Wein," COMICS JOURNAL No. 48, pp. 73-99

Wolfman, Marv
- "An Interview with Marv Wolfman," COMICS JOURNAL #44, pp. 34-51
- "The Total Marv Wolfman Interview, AMAZING HEROES #135, pp. 22-45

Magazines

Amazing Heroes
Comic Book Profiles
Comics Journal
Comics Scene
Famous Monsters of Filmland
Rocket's Blast Comicollector

Internet Sources

Comics 101: A (Brief) History of Comic Books in America
http://www.chs.org/comics/comics101.htm

Comics of the 1980s Homesite (Meesh)
http://members.tripod.com/~mister_meesh/index.html

Comixfan Forum
"PR: 'Nuff Said Plots Online at Marvel.com," posted 12/5/2001, http://www.comixfan.com/xfan/forums/showthread.php?t=12

GaryReed.net
"A History of the Comics Market,"
www.garyreed.net.Caliber/historycomics.htm

H. P. Lovecraft Archive
"Collected Essays, Volume 1: Amateur Journalism,"
http://www.hplovecraft.com/writings/sources/ce1.htm

History of British Comics
http://www.comicsuk.co.uk/History/HistoryLeft.asp

icv2.com
"Barnes & Noble.com Adds Graphic Novel Storefront,"
http://www.icv2.com/articles/home/2297.html

Nationmaster.com Encyclopedia:
- "American Comic Book": http:www.nationmaster.com/encyclopedia/America-comic-book
- "Comics": http:www.nationmaster.com/encyclopedia/Comics

Viz Media
- Shojo, http://www.viz.com/products/shojo/
- Shonen Jump, http://www.viz.com/products/shonenjump/

Correspondence

Cochran, Connor Freff
Cooke, Jon B.
Englehart, Stephen
Grell, Mike
Gold, Mike
Hester, Phil
Jurgens, Dan
Kitchen, Denis
Kuntz, J. Kenneth
Mennel, Timothy
Reed, Gary

FOOD FOR THOUGHT

I have been writing a long time and have learned that everybody is talented, original, and has something to say.
- *Brenda Ueland*

Writing, at least fiction writing, we must not forget, is nothing in the world but the most highly conventional form of picture painting.
- *William Foster-Harris*

There is no infallible guide to good writing, no assurance that a person who thinks clearly will be able to write clearly, no key that unlocks the door, no inflexible rule by which the young writer may shape his course. He will often find himself steering by stars that are disturbingly in motion.
- *E.B. White*

Good luck!

Be careful out there!

ART NOTES

Page 148: *The Sceptre* by Barb Jacobs © 1985

DID YOU LIKE THE ART IN THIS BOOK?
WHY NOT LET THE ARTISTS KNOW!

Christopher Jones
http://blog.christopherjonesart.com/

Jason Yungbluth
http://www.whatisdeepfried.com/tag/jason-yungbluth/

Sergio Cariello
http://www.sergiocariello.com/

Aldin Baroza
http://albaroza.com/

Rob Davis
http://www.robmdavis.com/

Barb Jacobs
http://barbjart.com/

S. Clarke Hawbaker
www.facebook.com/s.clarke.hawbaker

Robert Schnieders
Please contact Robert through www.caliber-entertainment.com

Craig Taillefer
http://www.craigtaillefer.com/

And while I'm not an artist, feel free to contact me at:
http://www.stevenphilipjones.com

INDEX

35123377R00085

Printed in Great Britain
by Amazon